THE COLLECTED WORKS OF

ERIC VOEGELIN

VOLUME 3

THE HISTORY
OF THE RACE IDEA
FROM RAY TO CARUS

PROJECTED VOLUMES IN THE SERIES

THE COLLECTED WORKS OF

ERIC VOEGELIN

VOLUME 3

THE HISTORY OF
THE RACE IDEA

FROM RAY TO CARUS

TRANSLATED FROM THE GERMAN BY

RUTH HEIN

EDITED WITH AN INTRODUCTION BY

KLAUS VONDUNG

LOUISIANA STATE UNIVERSITY PRESS

BATON ROUGE

Originally published in 1933 as
Die Rassenidee in der Geistesgeschichte von Ray bis Carus by
Junker und Dünnhaupt Verlag in Berlin
Translation and Introduction copyright © 1998 by Louisiana State University Press
All rights reserved
Manufactured in the United States of America
First printing
07   06   05   04   03   02   01   00   99   98   5   4   3   2   1

Designer: Albert Crochet
Typeface: Trump Mediaeval
Typesetter: Wilsted & Taylor Publishing Services
Printer and binder: Thomson-Shore, Inc.

The Editorial Board wishes to give grateful acknowledgment to those
who have contributed to support publication of this book and series
and especially to the Earhart Foundation, the Foundation for
Faith in Search of Understanding, the Windway Foundation,
the Liberty Fund, Inc., Robert J. Cihak, M.D., and John C. Jacobs, Jr.

Library of Congress Cataloging-in-Publication Data
Voegelin, Eric, 1901–
    [Rassenidee in der Geistesgeschichte von Ray bis Carus.   English]
    The history of the race idea : from Ray to Carus / Eric Voegelin ;
    translated from the German by Ruth Hein ; edited with an introd. by
    Klaus Vondung.
        p.   cm. — (Collected works of Eric Voegelin ; vol. 3)
    Translation of: Die Rassenidee in der Geistesgeschichte von Ray
    bis Carus.
    Includes index.
    ISBN 0-8071-1843-5 (cloth : alk. paper)
    1. Race—History.   2. Race—Study and teaching—History.
    3. Racism—History.   I. Title.   II. Series: Voegelin, Eric, 1901–
    Works.   1989 ; vol. 3.
    B3354.V8813   1989 vol. 3
    193 s—dc21   97-27027
    [305.8'009]   CIP

Contents

Editor's Introduction

"Let us now take a look at contemporary race theory," Eric Voegelin writes in the closing paragraphs of his introduction to *The History of the Race Idea.* "We will see an image of destruction. . . . It is a nightmare to think that we should recognize the people whom we follow and whom we allow to come near us not by their looks, their words, and their gestures, but by their cranial index and the proportional measurements of their extremities."[1] It is surprising that, with such unmistakable verdicts, Voegelin's book could still appear, by the end of 1933, within the borders of Nazi Germany.[2] It is no surprise, however, that National Socialist reviewers reacted with fierce, though utterly ignorant, criticism and that the book was available only for a short time.[3]

The History of the Race Idea forms a unit with *Race and State,* which was published earlier in 1933.[4] *Race and State* presented a systematic analysis of theoretical and methodological problems; it dealt with the formation of political ideas, in particular race ideas, their contribution to the constitution of communities, and the interrelationship between race and state. In his second book on race, Voegelin undertook a historical investigation of the race idea. In a memoir prepared in the late thirties for a possible English edition of the two books on race, Voegelin remarked, "*Die Rassenidee in der Geistesgeschichte von Ray bis Carus* is perhaps of lesser actual in-

1. Pp. 23–25 herein.
2. Published by Junker und Dünnhaupt Verlag, Berlin.
3. A selection of reviews can be found in Box 54, Eric Voegelin Papers, Hoover Institution Archives.
4. For the political and intellectual background of both *Race and State* and *The History of the Race Idea,* see my introduction to *Race and State,* Vol. 2 of *The Collected Works of Eric Voegelin.* A detailed exegesis of Voegelin's two books on race has been presented by Thomas W. Heilke in *Voegelin on the Idea of Race: An Analysis of Modern European Racism* (Baton Rouge, 1990).

terest than *Rasse und Staat,* but in my opinion the more important study from a scientific point of view."[5]

This historical study of the race idea spans a period of roughly a century and a half, from the late seventeenth to the middle of the nineteenth century. Voegelin did not bring the work up to the present because, in his opinion, this history was a process of deterioration, down to the condition of "decay" he ascribed to his time.[6] Already his introduction makes clear that the material he covers and the way he investigates it represent such high philosophical standards that the theories he deals with and the race theories accompanying National Socialism seem to have little more in common than the name.

It is one of the major achievements of Voegelin's study that the rise of the race idea is put into the context of the development of modern philosophy, and modernity in general, and thus made intelligible. The history of the race idea begins when the thought of a natural system of living forms first appears. And the main condition for the development of this thought is the gradual change from the Christian image of the human being to a post-Christian or pagan one. With this change, philosophy sets itself a new task: the "first goal is no longer the rational glorification of fundamental Christian experiences but insight into the nature of man."[7] Philosophy begins to oppose the former devaluation of "subhuman nature," and next, the devaluation of human existence in general, "insofar as it belongs to that realm by virtue of being a sensory-bodily existence."[8] Consequently, a new interest in "nature," including the physical nature of the human being, arises, and this interest leads to new insights. Intensified explorations of foreign parts of the world produce growing knowledge of the diverse bodily appearances of human beings, so that, toward the middle of the eighteenth century, the problem comes into focus "of the significance of the body and its diverse forms for an understanding of man."[9] Although the Christian idea of the human being as an essentially supernatural, imperishable substance is not discarded right away, the attempt now is made to place

5. Box 53, Eric Voegelin Papers, Hoover Institution Archives.
6. P. 19.
7. P. 5.
8. P. 6.
9. P. 7.

the human being with his variety of bodily forms within a systematic order of nature. In this context, the problem of race emerges as a particular case and, at the same time, as the epitome of the difficulties the new approach presents.

It is characteristic of Voegelin's detached manner of analysis that he refrains from direct value judgments regarding the epochal change from the Christian to the post-Christian or pagan image of the human being. This is in keeping with his epistemological position.[10] But he spells out unmistakably the consequences of that change; that the reader can easily draw his own conclusions is shown by some of the more intelligent and discerning reviews that appeared even as late as 1934. The renowned Catholic periodical *Hochland,* for instance, acknowledged as the main intellectual merit of Voegelin's study "that he discloses how race theories could gain their human and social importance only after the destruction of the idea of the *corpus Christi mysticum.*"[11] The *Blätter für Deutsche Philosophie* praised Voegelin for "work[ing] out sharply in detailed points" the transition from the traditional to the new view of the human being.[12] Voegelin himself took up the main issue once more in an article he wrote in 1935 for a volume of essays entitled *The Psychology of Community Life.* Here he characterized even more explicitly the significance of this transition: "The overthrow of the Christian cosmos is accompanied, in the soul, by a sharpened susceptibility to all sources of the atypical, the abnormal, the a-rational, the unordered."[13]

The History of the Race Idea represents, apart from its subject matter, and in the same way as *Race and State,* a further step in Voegelin's intellectual development. Again Voegelin deals with the general problem of how ideas originate and become formative for worldviews and for the social reality. In the introduction to the present volume he outlines his theoretical basis by distinguishing between *Urbilder,* literally "primal images," and *Denkbilder,* literally "images of thought." Primal images are products of a "primal way of

---

10. See my introduction to *Race and State,* Vol. 2 of *The Collected Works of Eric Voegelin,* xv.

11. *Hochland: Monatszeitschrift für alle Gebiete des Wissens, der Literatur, und Kunst,* XXXI (1933–34), No. 2, 185.

12. *Blätter für Deutsche Philosophie,* VIII, No. 2 (1934–35), 192.

13. Eric Voegelin, "Rasse und Staat," in *Psychologie des Gemeinschaftslebens,* ed. Otto Klemm (Jena: Fischer Verlag, 1935), 94.

seeing"; the Christian as well as the post-Christian or pagan image of the human being is such a primal image in Voegelin's eyes. These images have a direct influence on the social reality and may constitute communities and states by shaping the self-interpretation of their members without the mediation of a theory. Nonetheless, primal images are taken up also by philosophy and cast into theoretical images of thought. Primal images and philosophical images of thought correspond with and influence each other; they can be in harmony with each other but may also diverge widely. Voegelin developed this theory in order to accentuate the importance of the primal way of seeing and the independence of primal images from theories, and he stressed that, on the one hand, primal images do not describe reality analytically, and that, on the other, theories may be incapable of explaining certain empirical phenomena, for instance, the unity of body, reason, and soul.

Compared with his future philosophy of consciousness, Voegelin's theoretical approach here still lacks, to some extent, precision and differentiation.[14] But it is obvious that with his notions of "primal way of seeing," "primal images," and "images of thought," he was on the way to his future concepts of "primal experiences," "exegeses of experiences," and their "symbolization," with which he was able to more fully articulate the problem of how the immaterial reality of experiences is transformed by the consciousness into the material reality of symbols and of the precarious interconnection between these two modes of reality.

Nevertheless, the theoretical approach Voegelin developed for his historical investigation of the race idea was sufficient for an adequate and profound analysis of this subject. Voegelin maintained that the new way of seeing and thinking of the English zoologist and botanist John Ray was one of the main sources of the race idea. According to Voegelin's theory, Ray's new view of the natural essence of life produced a new "primal image" and, as a result, a new theory of species. It was Voegelin's discovery that Ray's theory, misunderstood and neglected in the past, became constitutive for the entire theory of the organic world in the eighteenth century up to Kant, and that it was much more important than Linnaeus' system.

14. For a more detailed account of the theoretical basis of Voegelin's two books on race, see Heilke, *Voegelin on the Idea of Race*, 7–35, esp. 24.

In the first part of his study, Voegelin traces this development of race theories and theories of species from Ray through Buffon and Herder to Blumenbach and Kant. In this context Voegelin makes clear that human beings have to be seen as *one* species that has spread all over the world,[15] which means that the different races must not be interpreted as being rooted in different species of early *homines*. By that Voegelin anticipated the most recent insights of genetics as represented, for instance, by Luigi Luca Cavalli-Sforza and Alan Wilson.

In the second part, Voegelin elucidates the development of the new concepts of the body, the "organism," and the person, from Ray and Leibniz to Goethe and Carl Gustav Carus. Again Voegelin emphasizes the precondition for this development, of which the formation of the modern race idea is just one particular part: namely, the new concepts of the body, the person, and the race presuppose a transfer of the existential center of the human being from the transcendent to the immanent realm. The transition from the transcendent to the immanent interpretation of life causes what Voegelin calls "an internalization [*Verinnerlichung*] of the body" and, parallel to this, "the internalization of the person."[16]

A decisive step along the way is the new meaning the term *organism* assumes in the philosophy of Caspar Friedrich Wolff (not to be confused with the more famous eighteenth-century philosopher Christian Wolff). Voegelin considers Wolff's theory of organism the most important biological theory of the eighteenth century insofar as it gives the term *organism*—which up to then was understood as meaning "mechanism"—its now common meaning. The new concept expresses the idea of a living substance that grows, regenerates, and reproduces according to an inner law, which is its own independent formative power [*Bildungstrieb*].

Voegelin characterizes the new concept of the organism as an "internalization of the body," because the formative power originally ascribed to a transcendent creator is according to this concept eventually attributed to the immanent body. An intermediary stage in this process is the "infinity speculation," which first tries to replace the divine act of creation by a structural law predetermined

15. P. 64.
16. P. 98.

xv

since infinity. Thus Voegelin explains the new concept of the organism as a special case of the general speculation on infinity, which runs from Leibniz' applications to mathematics and biology via Buffon to Kant's critique of antinomies. Voegelin demonstrates that with Kant the philosophy of living forms, including the theory of evolution, has reached a fully formulated theoretical standard compared with which the Darwinian theories of the nineteenth century must be seen as a decline.

By "internalization of the person," which runs parallel to the concept of the internalization of the body, Voegelin means the transition from the idea of the immortal soul to the idea of human reason in its infinite process of perfection. From here the final step is to the new finite image of the human being: "man as a productive unity of body and mind with a meaningful earthly existence."[17]

The emergence of this new image is interpreted by Voegelin as the emergence of a new primal image, first embodied in persons and then in corresponding images of thought. The new primal image of the person as an image of the "demonic" figure was pronounced most prominently by Goethe and Schiller.[18] In the *Sturm und Drang* period in which the theory of the "genius" was developed, the term *demonic* came to be used as an equivalent for *genius*. This understanding was initiated by Johann Georg Hamann, who interpreted Socrates' *daimonion*, his divine inner voice, as his genius; from that point on, the man of genius was understood as the "demonic man," especially by Goethe and Schiller. The demonic figure found its most distinct description, in Voegelin's eyes, as the "well-born man" in Carus' appraisal of Goethe. The image of the person as a body-mind unit in which both parts have equality provides the basis for Carus' theory of race.

In Voegelin's opinion, Carus' theory is the first great theory of race in the modern sense. At the same time, one could say it is the last, because, as mentioned before, the further development of race theories is characterized by Voegelin as a process of decline. Voegelin criticizes, in particular, the "complete ignorance of the classical state of the problem" in the biological and anthropological theories of his time.[19] This ignorance was caused mainly by the influence of

17. P. 16.
18. Pp. 10–11, 161.
19. P. 19.

Darwinian and post-Darwinian theories that, for instance, ignored Carus' concept of the well-born human being as a balanced unit of body and mind. The narrowing of this concept to apply only to particular physical conditions led, in Voegelin's words, to "the barbaric natural-scientific dogmatizations of modern eugenics."[20]

In his criticism of contemporary race theories Voegelin goes so far as to compare them with the basis-superstructure model of Marxism. Both doctrines subscribe to the fundamental thesis that consciousness does not determine existence but existence determines consciousness. In both cases the intellectual superstructure is seen as determined by material conditions—in the case of Marxism by economic conditions, in the case of race theories by biological ones. One of Voegelin's intentions in drawing the parallel between modern race theories and Marxism was undoubtedly to anger race theoreticians associated with National Socialism who prided themselves on their anti-Marxism. The main intention, however, was to dismiss *any* attempt to reduce the human being, his existence, appearance, and actions, to a phenomenon on a lower level: "Man as a spiritual-bodily historical substance cannot be 'explained' through something that is less than man himself, through his *physis*. Only man himself can create his sphere of action, namely, the historical community."[21]

20. P. 170.
21. P. 24.

THE HISTORY OF THE RACE IDEA

Foreword

This book presents the historical investigation of the race idea I promised to undertake in my systematic work *Race and State* (Tübingen, 1933). The two works supplement each other: whenever here, in connection with historical study, I touch on systematic questions, I have referred to *Race and State* for more detailed discussion; in that book I noted the analysis of this volume whenever questions of intellectual history emerged in the context of systematic study.

Vienna, October, 1933   Eric Voegelin

Introduction

§1. Primal Images and Primal Ways of Seeing

The knowledge of man is out of joint. Current race theory is characterized by uncertainty about what is essential and a decline in the technical ability to grasp it cognitively. We turn to the history of a great idea to trace the law of its creation in happier moments of the world-spirit and to return from this immersion in its mature forms with a new firm vision and with hands now more skilled to reproduce what we have seen.

The race idea came into being at a turning point in time; its emergence is an epiphenomenon of an extensive historical process characterized by a change in the primal image [*Urbild*] of man. There is no *one* primal way of seeing [*Urweise des Sehens*] and no *one* primal image of man maintained throughout history as the eternal norm of a perfect existence; the views and the images change with the times and nations. Though a law governs each new image, the change occurs freely; that is, we cannot fathom the ultimate reasons for the appearance of a particular image. However, we can understand the necessary conditions accompanying the first view and appearance of a new image and then trace the law of the course of its existence from its beginning to its decline and disappearance. A norm does not completely become an image unless it is realized in a historical person; and the image remains unseen in spite of its embodiment in a person if the time is not ripe for seeing it. Embodiment and fullness of time are the broadest categories of intellectual history under which we must look at the change in the image of man.

The primal images in whose transformation the race idea arises are the Christian one as it became flesh in the person of Jesus and a post-Christian, pagan one. Several persons have carried the development of the post-Christian primal image without any one so far having embodied it as decisively as Christ embodied the Christian one. The change is not marked by a sharp break, a clear end and a new beginning; rather, it is a blending of one image into another, a fading out of one and simultaneous intensifying of the other. The Christian image raises man out of nature; though it presents him as a creature among other creatures, as a finite being among others, it nevertheless juxtaposes him to the rest of nature; he stands between God and the subhuman world. This intermediate status is not determined by a unique formative law that would constitute man as a self-contained existence but by his participation in both the higher and the lower world. By virtue of his soul, man is united with the divine *pneuma*; by virtue of his body, his *sarx*, he partakes of transitoriness; his existence is "inauthentic" [*uneigentlich*]. The condition of his existence is that of being lost, an existence from which he must be freed in order to ascend to the realm of his true existence with his "authentic" nature. Man must live according to the example of Christ and follow Him: "Omnia vanitas, praeter amare Deum, et illi soli servire. Ita est summa sapientia, per contemptum mundi tendere ad regna coelestia." [All is vanity but to love God, and to serve him alone. Thus the supreme wisdom is to seek the kingdom of heaven by despising the things of this world.] It is vain to strive for riches, says the author of the *Imitation of Christ*, it is vain to strive for worldly honors and for a raised status, vain to wish for a long life. The world is vain, and the body a prison. The eye is not satisfied by what it sees nor the ear filled by what it hears; those who follow their senses lose grace. "Stude ergo cor tuum ab amore visibilium abstrahere, et ad invisibilia te transferre. . . . Quamdiu Dominum meum aperte in sua gloria non video, pro nihilo duco omne, quod in mundo conspicio et audio." [Take care therefore to withdraw your heart from love of what is visible, allowing it to center on things unseen. . . . As long as I do not see my Lord openly in his glory, I hold everything for nothing that I see and hear in the world.] The most important event in man's life is death; he must arrange his days with death in mind; he must seek solitude, flee from the sight and speech of other people, turn away from everything external and "intendere ad interiora et spiritualia" [turn to internal and spiritual things]. Every day is to be lived as if it were the last, and the soul should always be anxious for the world beyond the senses. Perfect calm of the soul can be found only in the eternal gaze upon God—"sed non est hoc possibile, durante me in hac mortalitate" [but this is not possible while I am in this mortal state]. Earthly existence is to be called "mortal," not because life ends in death but because the quality of *mortalitas* makes the whole duration of life something contemptible, unreal, from which the soul is liberated into a higher life, a higher reality. During his earthly existence, man connects with God in the act of communion; life after death no longer needs this expedient for union with God—"quia Beati in gloria coelesti non egent medicamine Sacramenti: gaudent enim sine fine in praesentia Dei, facie ad faciem gloriam ejus speculantes, et gustant Verbum Dei caro factum, sicut fuit ab initio et manet in aeternum" [because the Blessed in heavenly glory do not need the medicine of the Sacrament: for they are enjoying themselves endlessly in the presence of God, looking upon his glory face to face, and they taste the Word of God made flesh, as he was from the beginning and remains unto eternity].

Thus we have briefly outlined the image of man as Thomas à Kempis saw it in the *Imitation of Christ*. This can no longer be seen in the same intensity in the transitional period to a new primal image and on the intellectual level on which the race idea arises. What has remained as the essential trait is the devaluation of the subhuman world and of human existence itself as far as its creaturely transitoriness is concerned. At the same time, a correspondingly high value is placed on a soul substance that, freed from all worldly ties, leads an afterlife without death.

However, a philosophical anthropology whose first goal is no longer the rational glorification of fundamental Christian experiences but insight into the nature of man is more skeptically open to experiences transcending the horizon of Christian experience, and its own speculative movement leads it to doubt the validity of its constructions and to be willing to make attempts in other directions. As is characteristic for such transition times, we find in Kant experiences blending into each other that should be basic experiences, but for Kant they are no longer or not yet that. The undervaluing of earthly existence has remained from the Christian image of man—Kant considers it astonishing that philosophers could ever have come up with the idea that so imperfect and transitory a creature as man could ever fulfill the meaning of his life in his earthly existence and not need the hope of a life after death to perfect his faculties. However, the Christian idea of the coming of the Kingdom of God is so secularized that the kingdom of perfected man is envisioned as attainable on earth in an unending historical process; on the infinitely distant temporal horizon the kingdom evolved on earth and the one effected by God come together.

However, this raises the puzzling question why people today should have to lead such an imperfect life while those far distant generations will be allowed to lead a blessed life on earth—a question that cannot arise in the original Christian idea because there the heavenly kingdom is distinguished *toto coelo* from all worldly events. Kant, who sees the kingdom of heaven as a remote, earthly one, experiences therefore "astonishment" at the unequal treatment present and future human generations receive from divine providence. Though life in this world is imperfect, a perfect existence in turn can only be conceived as an earthly existence—an otherworldly life, after careful reflection, seems to Kant to be only an imperfect substitute for life on this earth. Kant's vacillation in his basic attitude to existence corresponds to the inner conflict in his thought system. We find the strictest separation of the eternal rational substance, which he sees as the true human nature, from the sensory dimension, which he considers a subordinate, evil realm, and, contrary to this devaluation of what is natural, we get the first full view of the phenomenon of organic life as an autonomous realm between mechanistic nature and the realm of reason.

In referring to Kant we are already looking at an advanced stage of the evolution of the race idea. Kant's system is the first step on the way to a reworking of an image of man increasingly distant from the Christian one—the vacillating attitude and the inner conflicts in the system indicate that a number of shattering blows must have been struck at the old image. Those blows were aimed at eliminating first the devaluation of subhuman nature and next that of human existence itself insofar as it belongs to that realm by virtue of being a sensory-bodily existence. As we have said, we can only record the concomitant circumstances of this process—its ultimate reasons remain beyond our understanding. Fascination with the enigmas of living nature may just as well be due to a new, extra-Christian experience of nature as to the desire to see divine providence at work even in the lowliest creatures. The attitude of the zoologist who sees the hand of God in the anatomy of a louse cannot be easily distinguished from that seeking to study the law of the living being without reference to divine manifestation. Here we are confronting questions of classification in intellectual history, and in our opinion there can be no unequivocal answer to them. Does the turn to a realistic look at nature represent a last lingering of Christian mysticism or a first step toward the new image of the world and of man?

We can, however, trace the course of this turn. The new understanding of living nature began with an enormous increase in knowledge of the subject matter in the seventeenth century and the first half of the eighteenth century; zoology and botany expanded their knowledge of living forms both in the number of genera and species and in the precision of knowledge about the structure of the various forms. Since the end of the seventeenth century there have been attempts to compile the knowledge of the large classes, such as birds or fishes, and to establish a system on which to base classification. The idea of a natural system emerged then as the first step to the subsequent effort at a historical classification of nature. We start with our investigations into intellectual history at these beginnings and show how the idea of a system is active in the works of the great English naturalists of the late seventeenth century, especially in those of John Ray, and how gradually the idea of a natural order of the living world came to prevail over the artificial order based on external characteristics, according to *genus proximum* and *differentia specifica*. Together with the knowledge of subhuman nature that of the physical forms of man also grew. Since the Renaissance, travel accounts, which had become more and more numerous up to the first half of the eighteenth century, had given a general idea of the variety in the bodily form of man, the broad outlines of which agree with our present-day knowledge.

Around the middle of the eighteenth century this collection of material had grown to the point of being ready for systematic classification, and thus arises the question of the significance of the body and its diverse forms for an understanding of man. Is man, as a being in nature, to be classified with the animals? How can such a classification be reconciled with the Christian idea of man as an essentially supernatural, imperishable substance? Is the variety of physical forms of any significance for man's soul and rational substance?

Is his essence to be defined as that of an animal species or as a unique substance radically different from animals? If the human substance differs radically from animal substance, what are we to make of the differences in customs, convictions, and institutions that go hand in hand with the physical differences, and so on? This problem was posed in the first systems of Linnaeus and Georges de Buffon, and its various possibilities have been explored by Buffon, Johann Gottfried von Herder, Johann Friedrich Blumenbach, and Immanuel Kant.

The new factual knowledge and the questions it raised gradually led to a readiness to see the living world and man in a new way. We can distinguish two phases in this maturation process: a first phase, in which the phenomenon of life appears as a primary phenomenon, and a second, in which an image of man as an earthly, self-contained, unified figure develops. In the first phase the Christian image of nature was dissolved. Plants and animals had been seen as creatures of God, as material beings shaped and ensouled by the hand of a master craftsman. The living substance presented itself as the medium in which a plan had been realized; organized matter was understood as a construct, a machine, an instrument embodying the ingenious idea of its builder and moving according to this idea.

In the eighteenth century this image of the machine was gradually changed into that of a substance carrying the law of its construction within it, a substance that is not created or animated from the outside but that is itself a primary force, a substance that is not given its life from the outside but lives out of the wellsprings of its own aliveness. It was not easy to focus on this phenomenon for the first time and to school others to see it. A thousand-year-old habit of seeing had to be destroyed, and a new one had to be acquired in its stead that was willing to accept living existence as primary and not to separate it into form and material. Buffon, Wolff, and Blumenbach had to persuade themselves and their contemporaries with the help of analogies to inorganic nature to accept what they saw as real. Nonliving matter as the building block of the world was the type of an independent and autonomous substance in analogy to which other independent substances could be conceived of. Starting with Buffon, we find attempts to substantiate the principle of aliveness [*Lebendigkeit*] by referring to the forces of matter—gravity and the force of attraction—until finally Blumenbach found the expression that convincingly designated the phenomenon of life as irreducible and incapable of combination: the formative drive [*Bildungstrieb*]. With-Kant's *Critique of Judgment* this first phase came to a close; life by then was understood as a primary phenomenon in its full extent, as life of the organic individual, as life of the species, and as historical unfolding of the whole living world. We will discuss this part of the process under the heading "The Internalization of the Body" because the image of the living being as one constructed from the outside out of matter and a planning power had changed into that of a substance living as a unified and self-contained one out of its own inwardness.

The second phase is one we have called the internalization of the person. When the image of life as internalized emerged, the Christian image of man as an immortal being chained to the sensory realm changed into the image of a unified figure living out its meaning in this earthly existence. Once again, as in the formation of the image of life, substantiating moments and the willingness to accept them as such had to combine. Just as the phenomenon of life became irresistible through increased knowledge of living beings in all their diversity, so the image of uniform man became obvious through its ideal realization in the great figures of the time. Frederick the Great, Napoleon, Grand Duke Karl August, and Goethe are the towering figures that served to train the vision of their contemporaries for what is unique and uniform in a human being. We find the traces of their influence everywhere. Kant had Frederick the Great in mind, but could not yet completely understand him. Though Kant no longer saw Frederick the Great as one figurant among many others in the development of human reason toward its perfection in the far-off future but rather as an excellent person outshining all other people, he could not yet see him as a unique phenomenon, a figure sufficient unto itself. Instead Kant integrated Frederick into his idea of development as its guarantor—this great figure was to guarantee that the development of reason was in fact progressing. However, the intuitive force and the aptness of expression, which could have substantiated what was seen, were still lacking—just as the view of the phenomenon of life was still incomplete without the symbolic force [*Zeichenkraft*] of the term "formative drive." After all, the new image could not be made visible within the imagination of a development toward the Kingdom of God and of the immortal rational substance imprisoned in the body.

9

Goethe and Schiller found the word that captures the powerful human existence in its earthly character [*Erdenhaftigkeit*]: the demonic. Soul and reason have a Christian hue—the soul is destined to suffer the trials and tribulations of earthly existence and ultimately to be redeemed; in accordance with the example of Christ, its existence is a Passion, not an action. Reason is the secularized bearer of the moral characteristics, of the virtues; it is the source of moral law and, its hue being more active, the source of the moral deed. The idea of the demonic, by contrast, consciously takes up pagan nuances; the sacred and the moral recede and the fertile, generative element ("the productive," in Goethe's terms) comes to the fore. For Goethe, the demonic nature signifies the great productivity that confers on works and deeds a condition of enlightenment, of grace; the demon is the ecstatic human being living entirely out of the center of a productive self, without tiring, without falling into periods of weakness—Napoleon is the primal image of a demon of action, Shakespeare of the demon of poetic works. Peter the Great, Byron, Mozart are listed as persons of great positive prolificacy and active energy, but the image of Napoleon always recurs, of Napoleon who followed deed with deed, whose life was filled to the brim with deeds, and who marched from one victory to the next like a demigod. The mark of productivity is not the quantity of what is produced but the intensity of life [*Lebensdichte*] that can be felt in all the expressions of the demonic man; he radiates a magic charm that is felt by everyone around him—it was so strong in Karl August that no one could resist him. "He attracted people by his serene presence, without having to make an effort to be kind and friendly." Radiant attraction and positive, active energy (Mephistopheles, the negative force, is not demonic) are meaningful in earthly life; they are bound to life and body; they are divine—but not in the Christian sense of a charisma bestowed on the elected soul. The well-formed body is an essential prerequisite for the effect of the demonic nature—a weak person cannot withstand the strain of ongoing and passionate activity. Once again Napoleon is the prototype: "Just consider all that *he* lived through and withstood; one would expect that by his fortieth year no part of him would have been left whole, and yet at that age he still stood there as a perfect hero." Demon and body here were still envisioned as active force and vessel or tool; happy chance, not necessity, have brought them together. Elsewhere Goethe elaborates the idea further and lets the demon take possession of the body; he speaks of the vivifying penetration of the body, of an ennobling of the body's organization by the demon, that makes it fit for great and ongoing activity well into old age. In the idea of a recurring puberty, spiritual and bodily elements interpenetrate, forming the idea of a spirit that undergoes bodily phases and of a body that rejuvenates itself in the phases of the spirit. Youth and old age are conditions of the body as well as of the spirit—an idea that is absurd in the Christian image of the indestructible, immortal soul.

The readiness to see the demonic element was (and still is) greater among Germans than among other nations, because the Christian image of man—for reasons of national history—was not expressed strongly in the image of the *homo politicus* and has therefore not shaped the area of civic-political action as strongly. Because of the inconsiderable traditional formal content of the civic-political sphere, the spirit was more free and willing to turn to new primal images; to examine the internalization of the person we have analyzed the German development of the image and the problem because there we find the phases of the change to the new image of man most clearly expressed. Just as for Goethe Napoleon was the most intense and prolific person, so Goethe represented the prototype of the perfect, this-worldly person for his contemporaries. In chapters 15, 16, and 17 we trace in detail the transition from Kant's still half-Christian image of man to the new demonic one. We have juxtaposed Schiller's ideas on the history of mankind to Kant's ideas so as to mark the point where they diverge; this divergence occurs at the point where Goethe comes into view as the earthly and present realization of what for Kant still lay in the far-off distance as the eternal kingdom of reason at the end of the world. In his perfect, self-sufficient worldliness Goethe confirmed for Schiller that a meaningful human existence was possible, even if at first only for small circles. Kant, on the other hand, was no longer entirely comfortable with the results of his escapist speculation on reason but could not tear himself away from the image of a soul that is perfected only in the next world. We will trace the understanding of the finite productive person in Humboldt's ideas and proceed from there to the perfect image of the uniform human figure Carl Gustav Carus saw embodied in Goethe—the person perfect in spirit and body, the well-born man, in whom mental health, prolificacy, physical handsomeness, and stamina combine and blend. This completes the primal image on the basis of which man's physical-spiritual unity will be understood in the future, and the race questions can be posed in their full scope, irrefutable and unshaken by arguments, because they are backed by the certainty of an image and a direct experience. Carus, who had the greatest ability for seeing things from the perspective of the new primal image, was the first to develop, compelled by the Goethean image, a more detailed race theory. Our study will conclude with the presentation of this theory.

§2. Thought Images and Types

By distinguishing between primal images and thought images, we break with the notion that philosophizing takes place only on the level of rational, conceptualizing science. While the philosopher forms concepts and judgments, these do not contain truth in the simple sense of an *adaequatio rei ac intellectus*; their meaning cannot be simply confirmed or denied as can that of scientific concepts and statements through a primary, revealing experience. Instead, the philosopher's concepts and judgments are evaluated based on two guiding criteria: intrasystematic consistency and the breadth and depth of the primal images that are to substantiate the total system. If the primal images and primal ways of seeing change, the philosophical thought images must change with them, and if the rational requirement for consistency within the thought images cannot be met, doubt spreads out from this failure and makes careful examination of a philosophy's primal images necessary. The change from the Christian to the post-Christian image of man is reflected in the sphere of thought images as a revision and reordering of fundamental philosophical concepts, which in turn speed up the transformation of the perception of the primal images.

In terms of thought images, our point of departure in this study is the necessity to create a conceptual apparatus for integrating the living substances, which became visible for the first time after the dissolution of the creationist view of the world, into a philosophical system. This raises the problem of the organism. In the Cartesian worldview, on which Buffon still based his thinking, the two fundamental classes of being are the disembodied soul and the soulless mechanism; now a new concept had to be found to appropriately de-

fine the living being having newly become visible, a conc€
would not simply describe the phenomenon with the help
Christian dualism of matter and soul. The eighteenth cent\
filled with efforts to create this new concept, which is finally d
oped through a change in the meaning of the word *organism*, most
clearly seen in Wolff's *Theoria Generationis*. We consider it one of
the most important results of our study to have ascertained the precise point at which the word *organism* took on the meaning we accept today as definitive and self-evident. Until the middle of the
eighteenth century, the meaning of the word *organism* was still
identical with that of *mechanism*, namely, a piece of matter constructed from the outside according to a plan. Thanks to the work of
Leibniz, Buffon, Wolff, Blumenbach, and Kant, the term gradually
took on the meaning of a living substance that develops, regenerates, and reproduces according to an inner law. The more clearly and
distinctly the living form appears as a primary phenomenon, the
more precise and definitive does the meaning of *organism* come to
designate it.

The concept of the organism, which was intended to offer a clear
view of the phenomenon of the living substance with its immanent
law of development, also marks the end of a heated discussion of the
species issue. The living being does not exist independently for itself but as a link in a chain, namely, the species, extending from the
past into the future through repeated procreation. In the Christian
view, the problem of the law governing the species was solved in the
same manner as that of the law governing the construction of an individual: by attributing it to the hand of a divine master-craftsman.
However, this solution is no longer satisfactory when faith in the divine creation of the world is shaken. For those who no longer believe
that the chain of species has a definite beginning at which its unique
characteristics were imprinted on it the species dissolves into separate individuals. As a result a peculiar transitional stage appears in
the history of ideas, one in which the image of a definite beginning
of the chain through divine design is already receding before the new
image has been established, the new image of a substance that carries its species characteristics within itself as its structural law—
which is then realized in the variety of individual forms. In this intermediate stage we find attempts at solving the problem with the
idea that the species-related law governing the structure of the indi-

vidual was predetermined from infinity. According to this idea, the structural law of the individual does not inhere in this individual but is determined by its predecessor in the previous generation, whose structure in turn was determined by his predecessor, and so on ad infinitum. The idea of the infinite replaces the divine act of creation, and for this reason Buffon embedded a profound analysis of the infinity issue in his biological-theoretical discussion, an analysis designed to prove that infinite regression cannot explain why here and now and at any arbitrary point in the sequence of generations the members of a species appear in an unvarying, constant form. Clearly, the structural law of the substance must always be present; it cannot be explained by regress to an authority situated outside the living form itself. We consider it the second most important result of our study of this topic to have shown the function of the infinity problem in the eighteenth century as a typical transitional problem between the finitism of the creationist worldview and that of the new post-Christian worldview. Speculations about infinity are not limited to Buffon's analysis or even to the field of biology but run through the entire century and through every single scientific field: from Leibniz—who posed the problem for mathematics, atomic theory, and biology—through Buffon to Kant's critique of antinomy and to the problem of infinity in history at the end of the eighteenth century.

The species problem brings with it the problem of evolution. Assuming an immanent law of the species is not an answer to the question of the beginning of the chain of generations. Knowledge of the diversity of forms draws attention to the relatedness of forms and to the possibility of arranging the species in turn in a sequence of historical origin. Speculation about the continuum of forms begins with Leibniz and ends with Kant's idea of the immanent evolution of the living world from the simplest forms to the most complex. The third most important result of our study is thus the explanation of the change in thought images to the idea of the development of species and their real descent from one another; this idea is supported by the first clear view of the primary phenomenon of the formal relatedness of all life and its historical development.

The analyses of the internalization of the person reveal the origin of the new concept of man in thought images. The problem of construction is the same as that arising in connection with the origin of the concept of the organism, and we can subsume both processes under the heading of change from the construction type of differential concepts to that of the unified form.[1] The construction type of differential concepts includes all attempts to understand the unity of a being, whether of a living being in general or of man, through the thought image of passive matter formed and animated by a principle allegedly essential to being. This construction type conforms most closely to the Christian primal way of seeing. Plants and animals can be understood as pieces of matter put together for a purpose, man as a transitory animal body with an immortal soul. Here the essence of being is located in the purposive plan, in the animal or human soul. We have called these concepts of being *differential concepts* because they are results of a process of subtraction: the passive part, the part fulfilling the function of matter, is subtracted from the total entity and what is left is the other essential and form-determining part. The structural plan of the living being, the plant or animal soul, is envisioned as dwelling in unformed matter, which we can directly experience as such in the processes of assimilation, in the elimination of inorganic matter, and in the phenomenon of death. In metabolism and the soulless body we see the building material that, for a time, is shaped by the animating principle and then falls back into its formless materiality. Thus, the essence of the form of being under consideration can be said to be the substance or principle that evidently remains after we mentally subtract the formless matter from the entity. Similarly, the human soul or spiritual substance can be elucidated in thought images, for example as the something added to the faculties man has in common with the animals that makes him human: man is animal plus spiritual substance. The Cartesian separation of bodily mechanism and soul and the Kantian distinction of the sensory nature and rational substance are further examples of this construction type.

The other construction type, that of the unified form, gradually came to prevail over the former as the primal images changed because it was better suited to the new way of seeing, which focused on the primary, independent, autonomous aspects of phenomena. The image of the organism replaces the thought image of the ma-

1. On the problem of types of construction, see the discussion in my *Race and State*, the chapter "Body-Soul-Mind."

chine, of the duality of matter and structural plan, or of the animated machine, the composite of artifact and animating principle. The image of the demonic figure or the well-born man replaces that of the rational being, the composite of sensory nature and rational person. In our study we have traced in detail the transition from the Kantian image of man and of history to that of Schiller because here we can see most distinctly how the new concept of man is defined as an intermediate one between non-sensory reason and non-reasoning sensory nature, how the concept of the beautiful life is defined as an intermediate one between the purely instinctual and the purely ethical life—just as earlier the organism was defined as the intermediate between bodiless soul and soulless matter. Even the details of the problems concerning the organism recur here on the level of the thought image of man: here, too, we find the analysis of the problem of infinity. Just as in creating the image of the organism the infinity problematic had to be replaced with a new, finite concept of organic substance, so here the ideas of the immortal soul and infinite progress in the development of reason had to be subverted until the new, finite image of man as a productive unity of body and mind with a meaningful earthly existence emerged. As the essential result of this concluding examination of thought images, we note that the speculative situations recur on the level of the thought image of man because the basic content of the change in thought images, the transition from the construction type of differential concepts to that of the finite unified form is the same here as on the level of the problem of the organism.

Let us take a look at the horizons the theory of primal images and thought images opens up for us. The constructions of thought images, we have noted, cannot be simply verified; they are not simply true or false but are attested to by the primal way of seeing to which they are integrated. These primal ways of seeing and the primal images they make visible also cannot be weighed against each other as to their truth content—they are all true, for they see what is real: the transitoriness of the sensory world, the experiences of death and of grace, these are all just as much experiences of something real as the experience of creative productivity and the certainty of living out a personal law in earthly life. The soul as the carrier of non-corporeal sacred and ethical values is just as certain as the bodiliness of all spiritual activity. There is no argument against a primal image—

even when such an argument is used, it aims not so much at demonstrating the correctness or falseness of a statement of fact as at defending its own way of seeing. To penetrate further into the laws of the development of primal images and their effect on people's minds leads us into issues of philosophy of society and of history. We see primal images arising through their embodiment in persons, and we see other persons willingly accept them and recognize them as exemplary ways of living out a human existence. We are faced with the historical fact that people have to varying degrees the character of primal images; rare men—Plato, Caesar, Jesus—have it to the utmost degree, and their images shine through the millennia; other people surround them in narrower and wider circles and receive the law of their lives from the primal image at the center; they may be more than mere followers and imitators and modify the primal image out of the wellsprings of their own aliveness and may themselves become a center, a model [*Vor-Leben*] for others—in an infinite interlocking [*Verschachtelung*] of circles and ranks, down to the closest connections of the present day and the example every living person is to all around him. Throughout history human society has been structured according to the effects radiating from the images of all ranks and ultimately from the great primal images; it has been structured according to the rising and falling of these images and according to the degrees of authenticity and inauthenticity with which people followed them (this seems to be a basic category in history, even aside from the special case of the *Imitatio Christi*) and quantitatively according to the groups and masses these images take hold of. The connections between images and their function in establishing, forming, and structuring society are the basis that ultimately gives legitimacy to the philosophizing about man. Here we can only hint at that great theme, which is only now coming into view—the theme of a sociology of philosophical thought.

It is thoughts of this sort that give meaning to the enterprise of a history of ideas. A presentation of philosophical propositions in chronological sequence may have value as a helpful accumulation of material—but it is not a history because it does not extend to the historical substance itself, to the lines of force in the connections among primal images. The thought images alone, separated from their historical ground, are bloodless shadows that have no effect on us and have nothing to say to us. Thought images aim to create a maximum of rational order in a world basically predetermined by the directions in which persons functioning as primal images open themselves to the possibilities of experiencing the world and also by the abundance of the individual experiences encountered in these given directions. Of course, the wealth of experiences may push one off the original direction, opening one's eyes to new possibilities: we need only remember how the accumulation of botanical, zoological, and ethnographic knowledge has led to the realization of the unique lawfulness in each sphere of being, something that had previously gone unnoticed because in the original Christian world attitude [*Welthaltung*] the experiences of transitoriness and salvation overshadowed all other world contents [*Weltgehalt*]. Or we need only remember the peculiarly vacillating attitude of Kant, which was determined, on the one hand, by his conviction of the shortcomings of human existence and, on the other, already colored by a sense of the meaningfulness of existence. The philosophical thought images do not stand alone but function as the rational organizing frameworks of a world structure shaped by primal forces.

§3. History and the Present

Our discussion covers a period of roughly a century and a half: from the late seventeenth century, when the thought of a natural system of living forms first appears, to the race theory of Carus, which was published as a memorial on the hundredth anniversary of Goethe's birth. This period and the events in it are delimited by the plan to present the primal images and thought images contained in the race idea in their genesis; we must therefore begin with the historical exposition of the problem of natural species, and we will end at the point where the image of the human body-mind unity has become established both concretely and conceptually. The further achievement of the race idea of constituting limited communities in history leads to questions of the formation of political ideas and to the topic of race and state, which I discussed in my book bearing that title. The selection of material within these limits was determined by my attempt to draw the lines of the connections between the primal images and the genesis of the thought images as clearly as possible. We have followed the transformation of the basic concepts through their intellectual pinnacles and have relegated a wealth of

18

material of lesser value to the background; the selection of the material was a matter of conscious judgment, excluding everything that would blur the large lines without enriching or adding color to the overall picture. We hope in this way to have restored the race idea in its original problematic, thus providing the basis for an assessment of its current condition and of the means to remedy it.

Compared to its classical form, the current condition of race theory is one of decay. The primal images have faded from sight, and the technical skill in forming concepts has deteriorated—aside from a few exceptions, today's race theory engages in inauthentic thinking about man. It is not our purpose here to criticize individual scholars and theorems; it is sufficient to refer to a few fundamental elements of the classical treatment of ideas to show convincingly the wide gap between then and now. The basic biological concepts of organism, species, and evolution were created as thought images in the eighteenth century, under the pressure of the direct view of life as a primary phenomenon. The whole problematic of these three basic concepts has in the main been worked out exhaustively. It became evident that they are connected with each other as signs for the life phenomenon in its three manifestations as living individual, as an order with a constant form, and as the historical unfolding of the living substance in a context of related forms. It was made clear, especially by Kant, that the parts of the phenomenon cannot "explain" each other—that is, the individual form cannot be "explained" by the species and the species cannot be "explained" by the evolution of form; morphologically and historically, life as a whole is a primary phenomenon. Today's biological and anthropological theory is characterized by complete ignorance of the classical state of the problem. The problem of species and evolution is discussed on the basis of Darwinian theory and the post-Darwinian development of science, which faces the speculative problems of the law of substance, the sequence of species and its beginning, the descent of species, and the beginning of organic evolution without a clue. In fact, almost a century and a half after the *Critique of Judgment*, there is an island where this work is unknown; where people have never racked their brains over the problems presented in that volume, and where people actually believe that the theory of evolution is a highly satisfactory explanation for something or other and that through diligent study of genetic laws one will not only learn the rules for the constancy of characteristics but also gain some insight into the phenomenon of life. The deterioration lies in the substitution of "theory" for the simple view of the primary phenomenon. We do not need a theory to tell us that organisms can be divided into orders with constant forms and that these orders in turn are morphologically related to each other—we can clearly see that much. Moreover, exploration of the earth's strata shows us the historical sequence of forms—we do not need a "theory" for all this. The desire for an "explanation" of the phenomenon arises when it is no longer seen itself, when eyes have become blind to the event of an autonomous unfolding of the living substance, when we look behind this law of evolution for another one more credible than the first. It is not this or that "theory" of evolution that seems to us more or less false, but the idea that any "theory" at all is needed. A "theory of evolution" can never do anything more than point out the external circumstances under which one form changes into another; nothing can explain the fact that a substance exists that has form or is capable of changing into another—here we confront the phenomenon we must accept unexplained. All attempts at explanation are fueled by the desire to reduce the phenomenon of life to a law of inorganic nature—or, to put it ontologically: they deny the reality of life and see only inanimate matter as the one primary phenomenon that has to explain all other phenomena. We are therefore not surprised that in spite of the enormous expansion in factual knowledge the history of biological *theory* since Darwin is the history of a fiasco. The explanation of the evolution of forms did not succeed, for the very good reasons we have just explained. Brighter minds no longer accept that one species evolved through the small steps of mutations out of another one, but even if evolution did take that path, this does not mean anything for the theory, for the problem of the law of life is not whether evolution took this or that path (it certainly has taken some path as we see in the results around us), rather, the problem is that living substance has a history at all and is subject to the law of development at all.

What is less clear to untrained minds is the fiasco of research on heredity. While the theory of evolution has quite evidently failed, genetics can nevertheless point to the fruitfulness of its way of formulating its questions and to the wealth of insight into the laws of heredity—here success seems to speak for itself. However, we must keep in mind that the laws of heredity are laws concerning the conservation of the form; the living form as such and the phenomenon of its invariance, by which the species is formed, are simply taken as givens, and research looks for the rules of hereditary succession for the form's components within the scope of these givens. The laws of heredity provide us not with a theory of living forms, but only with the rules of their material reconstitution in individuals of the same form; the law of the form itself evades their grasp. How far these studies lead us from the problems of life is clear when we consider that the rules of reconstitution of form in a succession of individuals come all the more into conflict with the historicity of life the more exclusively they are understood as *the* laws of the organic world. The modification of forms, the formation of new species is just as much a phenomenon as the invariance of form within a species; the more we concentrate on the one phenomenon, the more incomprehensible the other becomes. Though the factual results may be correct, nevertheless it is a mistake to believe that the law of form has been found, for even the species with its invariant form is subject to a historical law: the law of the unfolding of living substance in the succession of individuals with the same form. Literally and historically the individuals thus have to be understood as indivisible entities; by their nature they are living entities and not the jigsaw puzzle of hereditary factors they appear to be in genetics. The laws of heredity are not laws of form but, in our formulation, laws of material reconstitution. This is not to lessen their significance but simply to put it in the proper perspective. We undoubtedly owe them the insight into the hereditary transmission of characteristics, and we learn from them the consequences of the transmission of a sick *physis*. But this cannot blind us to the fact that the understanding of the living substance as it appears in individuals, in species, and in the entire world of forms has been dulled, and in fact largely been obliterated. This understanding has been replaced by a "theory" aiming to reduce the phenomenon of life to the laws of nonliving nature, and from this concept of inorganic law a malevolent, deadly fatalism, hostile to life and spirit, radiates into the higher levels of the world of organic forms and even into the higher one of the human form of body and spirit.

Because we have lost the primal way of seeing, in which the primal image of life presented itself as a historical phenomenon with its own lawfulness, because the phenomenon of matter has eclipsed everything else, the thought images of this material realm of being have covered up the ones the great thinkers of the eighteenth century have worked so painstakingly to create; in fact, they cover the latter so completely that even the knowledge of the great achievements of these men—particularly those of Leibniz, Wolff, Herder, Kant—has disappeared from the present. I tend to believe that there are few biologists today who know that the idea of the descent of species was enunciated by Kant and immediately examined as to its explanatory value.

All that is regrettable enough. It certainly does not confer honor on German science that most biologists and anthropologists are unfamiliar with the great German culture of theoretical biology. But we can look on all that as the internal affairs of a specialized science and, in view of the clear signs of disillusion and reflection, hope that this bad era will soon come to an end. However, these men, with no eyes for the brilliance of the German spirit, want to interfere in human relations and ultimately presume to explicate the German nation to us and to the world—an undertaking with evil consequences. For not only the primal understanding of the phenomenon of life has died away but also that of the image of man as great. When Schiller created his image of the sensory-rational man, the image of the demonic figure and the beautiful life, when Carus conceived of the idea of being well born, they were both thinking of Goethe, and under the influence of this primal image Carus developed his race theory. These thinkers saw the human figure as a unity, as body-spirit unity, but always as a human figure—that is, as the embodiment of a spirit. They would never have come up with the abstruse notion of pulling this unity apart and seeing the essence of the figure in the body without the mind. To be sure, the well-formed spirit needs a well-formed body to express itself fully, but the physical makeup by itself never reveals anything about the human-spiritual constitution of the person. Those great thinkers of the past would have been horrified at somebody finding in himself all the traits of the Nordic race with the help of a book on anthropology and then imagining himself to be somebody special who does not have to do anything else. In this area the decline of the primal images and thought images is disastrous. In the primal image of the demonic man one could see the great productivity, the uniqueness and mean-

ingfulness of the individual human figure. If the individual's historicity cannot be ignored in the sphere of the subhuman living world,
if it must already be clear here that the members of a species are not
interchangeable doubles and clones [*Doppelgänger und Vielfach-
gänger*] of one another, but that each individual is an irreplaceable
link in the total history of life, then it is even more important to see
also in man his historicity, for the specifically human community
connection lies outside the history of the species in the structuring
according to spiritual content on the basis of the physical connection. The fact that human beings are physiologically descended
from each other does not yet make a human history; that comes
about only when a human-spiritual, primal content manifests itself
in the physically related bodies. Everyone has a line of ancestors, but
not every ancestral line is a noble one, not even when it belongs exclusively to a race considered valuable. Only when a spiritual norm
keeps a rein on people and unites them does great history come
about; Plato established for all time the law of a noble body and a
noble spirit mutually requiring each other.

Let us now take a look at contemporary race theory—we will see
an image of destruction. Nothing has remained of the contents of
the primal images, and the thought images, which had made such
promising beginnings, have not been cultivated further. Everything
is to be understood on the basis of the primal image of matter; the
materialistic concept of laws has suppressed history; Carus' great
idea of man as well-born has been degraded to the concept of the eu-
genic, heritably healthy body—even if it is the body of a highly questionable person. Nothing has remained of Schiller's idea of the chosen circle, of Goethe's idea of the most intimate company; Stefan
George's new teaching of the spiritual kingdom has not been understood. The idea of the unity of mind and body, the will to see the demonic, well-born man as the center of others of the same kind, has
died away. What has remained of the great conception is the certainty that spirit is not a bloodless substance and that the body is not
an indifferent appendage of the person—but this certainty was broken by the liberal and Marxist ideas of the late nineteenth century.
*What unites the race theory rooted in this era with liberalism and
Marxism* is the will to deprive the state of history, to hand it over to
the masses, to destroy the historical substance and the primal image
of man in its community-forming function. To be sure, the liberal

ahistorical notion of human beings as equal exemplars of a species has been restricted; it no longer encompasses all of mankind, since not everyone bearing a human face is equal in the eyes of race theory, but the liberal idea is still strong enough so that everyone sharing a particular complex of physical traits is equal. Though Marxist materialism has changed in its content—for it is no longer the economic conditions that determine the spiritual superstructure but the biological ones—its basic thesis (not consciousness determines [bestimmt] reality, but reality [Wesen] consciousness) is not at all in doubt for the race theoreticians of this school. As in the case of the phenomena of life, a "theory" takes the place of the primal way of seeing. It is not enough that great men stand out because of their noble unity of body and mind, visible to all; they must be "explained." And as in the case of biological theory, the "explanation" consists in the reduction of the phenomenon of man to a phenomenon of a lower level, such as animals or inorganic matter. That the members of the community of noble blood come together out of the affinity between noble spirits, that the community is governed by its own laws of people finding and recognizing each other, of leading and following, of closeness to and distance from the center, of devotion and self-preservation, of radiant enchantment and acceptance without envy—to know all this and far more requires a primal way of seeing in which the full image of man is revealed. Man as spiritual-bodily, historical substance cannot be "explained" through something that is less than man himself, through his *physis*. Only man himself can create his sphere of action, namely, the historical community, which does not exist without men of strong imaginative force.

However, if we are blind to this reality and misunderstand the body-spirit unity as a duality of spirit and its bodily determinant, the dangerous thought arises that the historical substance could be arbitrarily generated by diligent clubs for the breeding of racially pure bodies—if only enough bodies of sufficient purity could be produced—then the result would not be bad at all! This gives rise to the dangerous superstition that the self-formation of the select community by the attraction of noble men to each other could be replaced by organization. And finally, most dangerous of all, the error arises that science could replace the innate certainty, honed through discipline, by which one man recognizes another as kindred or alien, as friendly or dangerous to his kind, that is, the faculty of reaction that holds a community together, regenerates it, closes it off and defends it. It is a nightmare to think that we should recognize the people whom we follow and whom we allow to come near us not by their looks, their words, and their gestures, but by their cranial index and the proportional measurements of their extremities.

Thus our turn to the history of the race idea is not merely meant as an extension of our horizon of knowledge; rather it serves the practical and scientific goal of recalling the basic questions of primal images and thought images that have disappeared from our horizon, to formulate them anew, and to challenge us to continue working on them. We admit that this work is not exactly easy to do; to become engrossed in the thought processes of a Leibniz, a Kant, and a Schiller requires effort, knowledge of facts, and a certain intellectual openness and willingness not everyone may rouse himself to—especially, as far as I can tell, not every race theoretician working today. We will not hold this against them, they may be excellent at performing the lesser services they are suited for—but then let them be silent regarding man and the state. Anyone who takes the easy way in matters of the mind [*geistige Dinge*] has no right to participate in this discussion.

PART I

SPECIES AND RACE
IN THE EIGHTEENTH CENTURY

1

Exposition of the Species Problem

§1. Linnaeus' Concept of Species

Linnaeus' biological theory of the fixity of the species is so superbly suited to serve as the point of departure for our investigations because of its persuasive simplicity. In a few lucid sentences the fixity of the living type is exhaustively formulated, and at the same time a catalogue of problems is presented that would be desirable in race theory today, since the modern studies are caught up in the difficulties of one or another subordinate detail and thus lose sight of the whole.

In his "Observationes" in *Regna III Naturae*, Linnaeus developed in a series of propositions the axioms of biology as he practiced it; and the first four of these propositions formulate the problem of species. The first proposition states the fact that all living beings emerge from an egg and that each egg produces a creature that resembles its parents. Linnaeus concludes from this that no new species are produced in the present time. The second proposition speaks of the multiplication of the number of individuals in all species through ongoing procreation; and from this he concludes that each species consists of a greater number of individuals today than it did in the beginning. In the third proposition Linnaeus traces this multiplied chain back to the original ancestor of each species (either a hermaphrodite or a pair differing in gender). The fourth proposition infers that since, first, no new species can emerge, and, second, like produces only like; and, third, the species is a unity—therefore the origin of those creative unities must be traced back to God.[1]

---

1. *Linnaei Systema Naturae*, 2d ed. (Stockholm, 1740). The "Observationes" are found on pp. 67ff. The first four propositions read:

1. Si opera Dei intueamur, omnibus satis superque patet, viventia singula ex ovo propagari, omneque ovum producere sobolem parenti simillimam. Hinc nullae species novae hodienum producuntur.

Thus the species are ontic unities and cannot vary; procreation is nothing more than the method for preserving these unities through the generations; the originator of these unities is God. The concepts and theses are forcefully and clearly formulated, and some of them are still part of the edifice of race theory in their original primitiveness. Thus the thesis of the immutability of hereditary unities is preserved in the principle of the constancy of racial types; it is the indispensable basis for the claim of the fateful consequences for man's spiritual and intellectual life that result from his belonging physically to a particular race. Through a strange concatenation of historical circumstances, in the prevailing popular opinion, the concept of the species and subspecies, after having gone through natural philosophy, Darwinism, and recent research in genetics, has once again arrived at the point where it was in Linnaeus' time. And the new attempts to interpret the phenomena of constancy and variation in such a way that the insight into the creative power of nature regains its rightful place have not progressed to the point where we would be

---

2. Ex generatione multiplicantur individua. Hinc (1) major hocce tempore numerus individuorum, in unaquaque specie, quam erat primitus.

3. Si hanc individuorum multiplicationem in unaquaque specie retrograde numeremus, modo quo multiplicavimus (2) prorsus simili series tandem in unico parente desinet, seu parens ille ex unico Hermaphrodito (uti communiter in Plantis); seu e duplici, Mare scilecet et Femina (ut in Animalibus plerisque) constat.

4. Cum nullae dantur novae species (1); cum simile semper parit sui simile (2); cum unitas in omni specie ordinem ducit (3); necesse est, ut unitatem illam progeneratricem, Enti cuidam Omnipotenti et Omniscio attribuamus, *Deo* nempe cuius opus *Creatio* audit. Confirmant haec mechanismus, leges, principia, constitutiones et sensationes in omni individuo vivente.

[1. If we grasp the works of God, it is more than sufficiently obvious to all that single living beings are propagated by an egg, and that every egg produces an offspring similar to the parent. Hence, no new species are produced every day.

2. Individuals are multiplied by generation. Hence (1) for any time period there is a greater number of individuals in any given species than there was originally.

3. Were we to enumerate backward this multiplication of individuals in any species, it is the case that in a manner utterly similar to that by which we have multiplied, (2) the series will ultimately leave off at a single parent, or that parent will be from a single hermaphrodite (as commonly in plants), or from a double, namely male and female (as in animals for the most part).

4. Since no new species are given (1); since similars always give birth to similars (2); since unity in every species leads to order (3); it is necessary to attribute that progenitive order to some omnipotent and omniscient Being, namely, *God*, whose work is called *Creation*. The mechanism, laws, principles, constitutions, and sensations in every individual confirm this.]

justified in speaking of a new post-Linnaean view of the living world.

What remains overlooked today is the problem of origins in this context. Linnaeus solved it with his thesis that God has created the life form and fixed it for all time, but since God as the originator of species and races is out of the question for any self-respecting modern scholar, these living unities must have "evolved." However, this brings up the phenomenon of variation which cannot be reconciled with the claim of strict constancy. It is not taken into consideration, however, that nothing is gained with the word *evolution* and that the beginning or origin of a succession of phenomena of the type of the living form is (1) a theoretical and speculative problem and (2) a metaphysical, real-ontological problem; at most, this is grudgingly admitted for the problem of the absolute origin of being.

§2. The Natural Method (Ray)

Linnaeus was so deeply convinced that God had created the species that the issue of an epistemological theory about the units of life and the methods for their description was only of secondary importance to him. He was convinced that the species were directly discernible and could be described adequately by indicating the one trait differentiating each from the *genus proximum*. In spite of the forcefulness and ambitiousness of Linnaeus' overall outline, a tendency to oversimplification of the problems makes itself felt in his position, a tendency that is all the more dubious as there were already before his time important studies (with which Linnaeus presumably was very familiar) of the epistemological and methodological questions involved. According to the prevailing opinion, Linnaeus was the "father" of systematic classification in botany, and because of his achievement as its creator one makes allowances for the flaws of the binary nomenclature and the rather superficial classification principle. Only on the basis of the beginning Linnaeus made, prevailing opinion holds, was our factual knowledge increased and the methods proved.

In fact, however, in the history of science a continuum of a more profound treatment of the species problem and of the scientific method begins long before Linnaeus and extends in its tradition far beyond him. In this continuum, Linnaeus' work stands out almost as an alien element; only a few relevant points, such as the constancy of species, are also found in his work, but the detailed and precise work on epistemology and methodology carried out by earlier and contemporary scholars meets with no response in his work. From the works preceding Linnaeus, I will single out for our purposes the significant foundational works of John Ray and Francis Willughby. They encompass the whole topic of eighteenth-century biology in its basic outlines and so provide us with the best exposition of the issue of biological species and races, which forms the underpinning of modern race theory.[2]

Willughby, a zoologist, and Ray, a zoologist and botanist, dealt decisively with the problem of classification and the adequate description of a unit of life, the one (Willughby) primarily in practical work through his typology of species, the other (Ray) also in theoretical discourses. The problem of species unity makes itself felt as a problem in the concrete difficulties in the proper differentiation of species. In the foreword to Willughby's ornithology, Ray justifies the descriptive method applied in this work, calling the reader's

2. The work of Willughby and Ray, especially Ray's, is largely ignored nowadays. For the eighteenth century, it was of the utmost significance. Even Linnaeus refers to it explicitly, though he makes no use of the possibilities it offers for the formulation of theories. In the "Observationes" of the second edition of *Systema Naturae*, concerning the animal kingdom, Linnaeus writes, "Paucissimi vero sunt, qui Zoologiam in Genera et Species secundum leges Systematicas redigere tentarunt, si Willughbeium et Rajum excipiamus" [With the exception of Willughby and Ray, very few indeed have tried to reduce zoology to genera and species in accord with systematic laws] (p. 75). Even during the time of Kant, Ray is cited as the authority for the development of the biological concept of species. Girtanner writes, "Several famous naturalists have already tried to define the species according to the laws of reproduction, or have at least acknowledged the correctness of the principle that animals who together beget fertile young belong to one and the same physical species. For example, Rai, Frisch, and Büffon" (Girtanner, *Über das Kantische Prinzip für die Naturgeschichte: Ein Versuch, diese Wissenschaft philosophisch zu behandeln* [Göttingen, 1796], 4).

What Em. Rádl writes in his history of biological theories since the end of the seventeenth century (Part I [Leipzig, 1905], 130–32) about Ray strikes me as completely inadequate. The fault may lie in part in the fact that Rádl was not familiar with all of Ray's works; but even what he says, probably on the basis of the works he cites, leads me to suppose that he did not know how to read Ray. According to Rádl, "little that is theoretically new" can be found in Ray's views; he belongs to "the class of scientists that reached its zenith with Linnaeus; those scientists cared less about immersing themselves in the biological problems through independent reflection than to work as broadly as possible": Ray "mainly influenced the shallow systematics of the eighteenth century, among others especially that of Linnaeus." Compare these claims with what I have to say in the text that follows.

attention to the fact that the species are defined by complexes of traits whenever the usual scholastic practice of description by a single trait, the *differentia specifica* in the more concise sense of Aristotelian logic, seemed insufficient.[3] This statement already distinguishes between the scholastic system and the natural system in Kant's sense, though without giving it a name yet. In the classification according to scholastic logic the species is characterized through the identification of the specific (in the logical sense) trait distinguishing it from the *genus proximum*. By contrast, Ray has a real-ontological concept of species as it exists in nature; in view of this reality of a species, the scholastic system of distinguishing traits can fail. The practical needs of a more concrete science lead to the emancipation from a method that formulates its rules according to the scholastic doctrines of *genus proximum* and *differentia specifica:* traditional logic is replaced by a method that follows closely the structure of its subject. Nature with its species itself becomes the guideline for the method of typology. In the subtitle of Willughby's later *Historia Piscium*, this idea is formulated in principle. There we read that in these four books fish in general will be discussed and that there will also be a description of all species, according to a method that follows the guidelines given by nature.[4] The method here becomes the servant of nature and follows its lead.

In a somewhat later work on botany, Ray attempts to justify his classification of plants into trees and herbs, a classification that was new and unusual at that time. As he put it, according to the consensus of contemporary botanists, the objection will be raised that the *notae characteristicae* of the genera and species should be based on

3. *Francisci Willughbeii Ornithologiae libri tres*, ed. Joannes Raius (London, 1676), foreword: "Sin vero in aliqua specie nihil singulare occurreret, quo ab aliis posset distingui, partes omnes accurate descripsit, ut saltem collectio multorum accidentium, quae simul omnia in alio quocumque animali non possent reperiri, pro characteristica esset." [But if in some species nothing singular were to occur by which it would be able to be distinguished from others, he describes all the parts accurately, so that at least a collection of many accidents, all of which would not be able to be found at once in any other animal, would function as the characteristic.]

4. *Francisci Willughbeii De historia piscium libri quatuor*, ed. (posthumously) John Ray (Oxford, 1686): "Sed et species omnes, tum ab aliis traditae, tum novae et nondum editae bene multae, naturae ductum servante Methodo dispositae, accurate describuntur." [But also every species, both those handed down by others, and many not yet well set forth, drawn according to the method of nature's disposition, shall be accurately described.]

the differences and similarities of blossoms and fruits, to which he replies that the traits of blossoms and fruits are very useful for defining subdivisions, but that the principal divisions must be guided by the total habitus.[5] The total habitus, or total constitution, which can be described only by a complex of traits, is thus introduced as the element guiding the definition of types; the natural unit as a real unit becomes almost tangible in this idea as opposed to the arbitrary system. The idea is summed up (decisively) in the statement, "Methodum intelligo Naturae convenientem, quae nec alienas species coniungit, nec cognatas separat." [I understand a method that agrees with nature, that neither joins alien species, nor separates cognate ones.] What Ray has in mind is a system adapted to nature; he concedes almost contemptuously that over against this "natural" system, artificial ones can arbitrarily be established and every plant can be assigned a place in them, but they contribute nothing to our knowledge of real divisions in nature.[6]

§3. Natural System and Scholastic System (Ray to Kant)

From these beginnings, Ray's *Methodus Plantarum* penetrates the problem most deeply. The concept of the total habitus had been at-

5. Joannes Raius, *Stirpium Europaeorum extra Britannias Nascentium Sylloge* (1694), "Praefatio": "Dices, unanimi Botanicorum huius saeculi consensu ratum esse, notas plantarum characteristicas generum discretivas, et specierum constitutivas, a florum et fructuum convenientiis et differentiis sumi debere. . . . Respondeo, me notas hasce a Flore et Fructu desumptas ad Genera subalterna discriminenda utiles esse concedere: primarias autem Plantarum divisiones, a toto earundem habitu et constitutione, aut insigni aliqua proprietate potius desumendas esse existimo, unde et ligneam etiam substantiam pro Nota admitto." [You may object that it is the unanimous consensus of the botanists of this century that the characteristic marks of plants, by which genera are discriminated, and that are constitutive of their species, ought to be drawn from the similarities and differences of flowers and fruits. . . . I respond that I concede that such characteristics drawn from flower and fruit are useful for discriminating subalternate genera: I contend, however, that the primary divisions of plants must rather be drawn from their bodily condition and constitution as a whole, or from some outstanding property, whereby I also admit woodiness of substance as a characteristic.]

6. *Ibid.*: "Alias enim si vel florum tantum vel seminum et vasculorum seminilium convenientias et differentias respiciamus, divisionem institui posse concedo, cuius membra omnia absque medio contraria sint, ita etiam ut nulla omnino detur species quae sub eorum aliquo non contineatur." [For if we regard other similarities and differences, whether of flowers alone, or of seeds, or of seminal vessels, I concede that a division can be established, all of whose members are contraries without a middle, so that no species whatsoever is given that is not contained under some one of them.]

tained, and this phenotypical habitus, whose traits can be summarized as a type, was now understood as the expression of a life unity,
a vital essence. Outwardly, the way it is defined still follows the
traditional logical forms: "Definitio perfecta conficitur e Genere
proximo et Differentia essentiali" [A perfect definition consists of a
proximate genus and an essential difference]—but the *differentia
specifica* has been replaced by the *differentia essentialis*. The
species-distinguishing trait was traditionally understood as a trait
of the phenotype pure and simple, but the essential characteristic
is for Ray the manifestation of an essence behind the appearance.
"At essentiae rerum nobis incognitae sunt, proinde et Differentiae
earum essentiales." [But the essences of things are unknown to us,
inasmuch as their essential differences are.][7] The real-ontological
concept of essence is introduced to contrast on the linguistic level
the real natural life unity with the concept, weighed down by logic,
of the species, and the expression *differentia essentialis* has the
function of relating the individual trait to the life form in which it
appears, while the *differentia specifica* points to the position of the
concept in the logical system of classification. Thus, the contrast between the descriptive-classifying concept formation (the scholastic
system, in Kant's language) and the research guided by the natural
divisions (Kant's natural system) appears even on the level of terminology. In fact, it has been claimed that Ray also formulated the criterion of a natural division: the interfertility of supposed individuals
to belong to the same subdivision.[8] If this is true, then Ray's theory
would have already contained all the ideas that served Kant as the
basis for his uncommonly drastic statements on the essence of the
life form. And these statements by Kant, in turn, pursue the possi-

---

7. John Ray, *Joannis Raii Methodus Plantarum emendata et aucta: In qua Notae
maxime Characteristicae exhibentur, quibis stirpium Genera tum summa, tum in-
fima cognoscuntur et a se mutuo dignoscuntur* (London, 1733; first published in
1703).

8. For this claim, see the above-cited passage in Girtanner's application of the
Kantian principle. Further, Blumenbach, *De generis humani varietate nativa*, 3d ed.
(1795), 67: "Raius quidem, vir immortalis, praeterito iam saeculo, adeoque diu ante
Buffonium ea animantia ad eandem speciem referenda esse censuit, quae invicem
coeant et foecundam prolem gignant." [Indeed Ray, an immortal man of the last century, to an extent long before Buffon held the opinion that these animating entities,
which mutually cause each other and bring about fertile offspring, be referred to as of
the same species.] However, none of the authors documents his statement with a
source, and I myself have not found an unequivocal formulation to this effect in the
works I have read and cited here.

bilities inherent in these fundamental ideas to the point that current biological theory, insofar as it deals with them at all, has nothing really new to add.

Kant distinguishes between the scholastic classification of phenomena and the other type of classification that is based on the natural divisions. The interfertility of individuals determines whether they belong to the same natural division, a principle ascribed to Ray and for which Kant draws on Buffon. Scholastic classification concentrates on classes according to similarity, while natural classification arranges phyla according to kinship: "the former intends merely to subsume creatures under headings, but the second wants to place them under laws."[9] The designation of natural subdivisions is thus simplified significantly compared to the Linnaean system; the distinction between genera and species disappears, and the term *phylum* designates the individuals who belong together according to the above-mentioned criterion; all larger groupings are artificial. The variations within the phyla are divided into *races*—hereditary varieties—and *variations*—differences that are not necessarily hereditary.

This was the precursor of the modern system of species, mutations, and variations, though it was not yet as clearly defined because the facts of genetics were not yet known. The individual natural divisions, the phyla, are constant, as were the Linnaean species, and the races developed within the phyla through the unfolding of dispositions that were present in seminal form in the as yet undifferentiated phyla. The potential of developing in one or another direction was already present, but it was realized only when particular external conditions occurred, which then favored the unfolding of one potential while allowing others to wither. This explains why the races we find today can no longer regress to their undifferentiated phyla or develop in completely different directions. There is obviously a close kinship between this theory and Heinz Woltereck's most recent studies[10]—in both, a natural division, the species, is

9. Immanuel Kant, *Von den verschiedenen Racen der Menschen: Zur Ankündigung der Vorlesungen der physischen Geographie im Sommerhalbjahr, 1775* (Philosophische Bibliothek), 87.

10. See Heinz Woltereck, "Vererbung und Erbänderung," in *Das Lebensproblem* (1931). Further, Woltereck, *Variation und Artbildung* (1919). Compare my book *Rasse und Staat* (1933), 49–53.

considered the smallest, so far at least, biological division, and both theories interpret hereditary mutations or races as unfoldings of what was already inherent in the nature of the phylum. To use Woltereck's formulation, the viable hereditary traits are already predetermined through the reaction norm of the species; mutations beyond the boundaries of the species' constitution are not possible.

Kant is exemplary in his further application of this principle of interpretation to the variations down to the individual level, a part of the theory completely lacking in modern race theories—not because of the subject matter, but only because of the authors' deficient theoretical background. Even in the personal variations nature does not proceed in complete freedom, but according to Kant, just as in the case of race characteristics, nature develops the original predispositions of the phylum. "The variety among people of the very same race was, in all probability, as effectively inherent in the original phylum in order to establish and subsequently develop the greatest diversity for an infinite variety of purposes, as the difference between races was present to later develop into fitness for fewer but more essential purposes."[11] Race is not the ultimate determinant of the individual phenotype; rather every one of its traits must be regarded as the direct unfolding of the predispositions of the human phylum. The possibilities of human nature are spread out before us in the infinite variety of individual forms. That individual characteristics are not heritable Kant takes as an indication that nature "does not want the old forms always replicated but instead desires the expression of all the variety it had embedded in the original germs of the human phylum."[12]

In the field of biology (there is nothing similar in anthropology) it is once again Woltereck who comes closest to this view. For him the variations are also determined by the reaction norm. Kant, however, goes further and (more important for anthropology than biology) develops the idea of the bodily singularity of each person, so that only the human species as a whole can express the human essence in bodily form through all its individuals throughout history. Kant cites the physiognomical uniqueness and inner unity of every hu-

11. Kant, *Über den Gebrauch teleologischer Prinzipien in der Philosophie* (Philosophische Bibliothek, 1788), 154.
12. *Ibid.*, 154.

man face, thus transferring the problem of singularity from the merely physical sphere into that of spiritual expression. The idea of the singular body-mind unified person is almost attained here, though not yet completely—for reasons we will discuss in greater detail in subsequent chapters.

Having followed the consequences of the natural system as opposed to the scholastic system up to this point, we will now return to Ray's ideas, with which we began.

§4. The Essence (Ray to Goethe)

We have followed Ray's idea of distinguishing between the real essence and the classificatory species to Kant's ideas on the scholastic and the natural system. In Ray's theory there are relationships between the essence of a living form and its traits that lead into epistemologically significant problems. The essence lies somewhere "behind" the traits meeting the observers' eyes and guiding their ordering of the phenomena. In one of its meanings this "behind" covers a causal connection between the invisible essence and its manifestation, the phenotype. This connection is the key to understanding the essence itself. Since only similar traits and functions flow from a particular essence, the fact that several individuals share the same habitus can be interpreted as an indication that they also share the same essence.[13] Such likeness in habitus, texture, and appearance is the sufficient guarantee for identity of essence; the possibility, however, that an isolated trait can be considered essential is deemed improbable.[14]

The concrete, visible overall habitus of the living creature is the

13. Ray, *Methodus Plantarum*: "Verum cum ex eadem essentia eaedem qualitates, operationes, aliaque accidentia fluant, non alia certior convenientiae essentialis, seu genericae nota esse potest, quam plura habere attributa communia, seu plures partes et accidentia similia, vel totam faciem, habitum et texturam eandem." [But when the same qualities, operations, and other accidents flow from the same essence, there cannot be noted anything of more certain essential or generic similarity than to possess many common attributes, or many parts and similar accidents, or the same whole face, appearance, and texture.]

14. *Ibid.*: "Proprium enim accidens, quod soli alicui generi omnibusque sub illo contentis speciebus conveniat, quod pro differentia essentiali ubi desideratur, adhibendum statuunt Dialectici, paucissimis conceditur." [For the proper accident, which agrees with only some genus and with all the species contained under it, which the dialecticians state ought to be used for the essential difference as desired, is conceded by very few.]

expression of a unity working in the background and itself remaining invisible. In this contrast we find the same problem dealt with in contemporary biology under the heading of gene structure and the traits expressed in the phenotype. In both the phenotype is determined by a causal factor whose qualities cannot be seen but must be deduced. This causal analysis ultimately leads, as we see in Woltereck's work, beyond the sphere of material determination to the reaction norm [*Reaktionsnorm*] as the determining "inextensive diversity"—that is, an entity that can no longer be comprehended by means of mathematical-scientific analysis and thus leads us back to the living unity as one we have "seen" with our eyes.

We find the ambiguity inherent in the concept of the reaction norm also in Ray's concept of essence. Just as Woltereck's reaction norm is the causal determinant of the phenotype and at the same time because of its inextensivity leads us back from the causal analysis to the reality of organic essence accessible to intuitive perception, so Ray's essence also signifies both the cause of the organic form and its host of traits and the seen being of the living creature, which guides the selection of traits with which the living being is to be described "essentially," "naturally" (in contrast to the scholastic classification according to arbitrary traits that are irrelevant to the natural subdivision). In discussing this problem, Ray arrived at formulations we will hardly find in modern biology but meet with in the humanities in the typology of Max Weber and Georg Simmel. The total habitus characterizing the living being must be conceived of in the concept of the type, and according to Ray this concept of the type is legitimately formed even when the individuals subsumed under it differ quite significantly from each other in various traits. The traits are selected on the basis of an immediate grasp of the object, and the selected group is considered "typical," while other traits and groups of traits may be ignored as being "inessential" and should not be considered characteristic. The formation of types thus is the result of a value-based selection (in the sense of Heinrich Rickert's logic of history), which in this case means: a selection is made in which the guiding "value" is the directly grasped vital essence of the plant.[15]

15. *Ibid.*: "Quocirca Plantas, quae plures partes et accidentia similia habent, totove habitu et textura conveniunt, quamvis Floris figura, eiusve petalorum numero,

The "ideal type" so arrived at does not comprise a group of traits an individual absolutely must possess to be considered a member of the type; rather, the traits are ordered with a view to the concrete essence. The empirical specimen may be more or less close to the essence, and perhaps no individual ever fully attains this essence. That does not make the type formation orientated to the concrete essential unity any less legitimate. In the eighteenth century and in biology, this problem of the visibility of the living essence found its classical expression in Goethe's statements on osteology. According to Goethe, in establishing the type, we

are assured by the nature of the undertaking that our procedure is not merely hypothetical, for in looking for laws according to which living, separate beings, acting out of themselves, are formed, we are not getting lost in vast breadths but are being taught on the inside. That nature, when she wishes to produce such a creature, must concentrate its greatest diversity in the most absolute unity is evident from the concept of a living, definite being, separated from all others and acting with a certain spontaneity. So we consider ourselves already assured of the unity, diversity, expediency, and lawfulness of our subject. If we are now circumspect and strong enough to approach our subject with an imagination that is simple yet wide-ranging, free yet guided by its own laws, lively yet regulated, to observe it and deal with it; if we are able to meet the certain and unambiguous genius of creative nature with the complex of spiritual powers we usually call *genius*, but which often produces very ambiguous effects; if several persons could work on the enormous subject with a common purpose; then surely the result would have to be something we as human beings should delight in.[16]

---

semine nudo vel vasculo incluso, cellularum, in qua dividitur eiusmodi vasculum, numero, aliove quocunque accidente differant, ad idem genus reducere non vereor." [As regards plants that have many parts and similar accidents, or whose entire appearance and texture are in agreement, even though they may differ in the shape of the flower, or the number of its petals, in its naked seed or with vessel included, in the number of cells in which the vessel of the same kind is divided, or in some other accident, I do not hesitate to reduce them to the same species.]

16. Johann Wolfgang von Goethe, *Osteologie: Vorträge über die drei ersten Kapitel des Entwurfs einer allgemeinen Einleitung in die vergleichende Anatomie, ausgehend von der Osteologie* (1796), second section.

An amusing anecdote by Justus Möser indicates that in those days an understanding of the methodological issues was not lacking and in fact hit the nail on the head even in out-of-the-way areas, free of the inhibitions associated with the basic metaphysical questions. In this selection the problem of the ideal type is thoroughly articulated by a sensible wine merchant: "Wouldn't that be the something! I retorted, and took the glass sitting on the table before me: This wine here is a Markobrunn from 1759, and *if it had something else and didn't have this*, it would be the best Markobrunn I ever drank. . . . So I want to imagine for every sort of Rhine wine not only the

Ray's theory of the living unity and its essence contains the full scope of the speculative problems—the scope that allows them to be carried to the poles of Kant's causal analysis in the natural method and Goethe's biology that sees the essence itself.

§5. Further Illumination of the Species Problem (Ray)

The same calm, objective consideration of things characterizes Ray's theories when he deals with the ramifications of the species problem. We can further illuminate [*auflockern*] the problem of species and expand the catalogue of subsidiary questions by following Ray's investigations in his *Discourses* because they differ from the contributions of contemporary and later authors in not defending specific theses but, taking the position of an empiricist, leaving the questions open. The problems are posed but not "solved," and they thus retain the full scope of their tension. Linnaeus did not doubt that every species is descended from an original ancestor created by God; Ray sees several possibilities, but all are still within the framework of the biblical creation story. First, Ray leaves undecided whether God created the seeds that were developed by the elements (thus initiating the chain of reproduction) or whether there were complete animals in the beginning and God gave every species "a Power to propagate the like." Moreover, the question remains whether at the beginning of the species there was one pair or many similar pairs. The analogy of the creation of man and woman and the story of the Flood, where a pair of every species was sufficient, Ray argues, would point to monogenesis. On the other hand, the biblical account reporting the creation of an abundance of animals and the difficulty the monogenetic theory has explaining the distribution of many animal and plant species speak for the other possibility. Thus, biblical arguments are joined by empirical ones, opening up the question of monogenesis and polygenesis (at that time only in regard

---

highest degree of excellence, but also, because you're talking about artistic ideals, the most perfect wine ideal in Rüdesheim, Hochheim, Laubenheim, and, in short, in all our wines; I want to taste the wines as if I had really drunk them that can be pressed from our grapes all the way from the Cape to Westphalia." Justus Möser, "Über das Kunstgefühl: Von einem Weinhändler" (1780), in *Patriotische Phantasien*, Vol. IV of *Sämmtliche Werke* (10 vols.; Berlin, 1842–43), 11.

to the nonhuman living world) that played such an important part in the race theory of the first half of the nineteenth century.[17]

Ray also expresses doubts on the question of the appearance of new species in modern times. While Linnaeus was certain that all species had been created in the original act of creation of the world, Ray leaves open the possibility of a later appearance of species and argues that any newly appearing species is also necessarily the product of a creation.[18] For Ray the problem of the creation of new species is not all that different from that of generation since in both cases new living beings are formed out of matter. Nevertheless, for Ray the possibility that every act of procreation represents a direct, creative divine intervention does not turn into a thesis excluding all other possibilities. Rather, in his cautious way, he leaves the question undecided and does not exclude the preformation of creatures as impossible. The individual of a species might very well be preformed in the egg and even contain its preformed descendants, resulting in an infinite encapsulation of all individuals back to the first individual of a species, which contains preformed within itself all those who follow. Ray dispels objections based on the unimaginable smallness of the germs by pointing to the infinitely small animals observed with a microscope, to the enormous staining power of infinitely tiny amounts of copper sulfate, to the fragrance emanating from ambergris that occurs without noticeable weight loss, and other examples of tiny particles having big effects.[19] These arguments, too, are not pursued to the point of putting forth a dogma of preformation, but are left as conjectures.[20] The only thing Ray

---

17. John Ray, *Three Physico-Theological Discourses: Concerning, I. The Primitive Chaos and Creation of the World; II. The General Deluge, Its Causes and Effects; III. The Dissolution of the World and Future Conflagration,* 4th ed. (1732; 1st ed., 1693), 45ff.

18. *Ibid.,* 48: "What did *God* at the first Creation more than, if this be true, we see every day done, that is, produce a new Animal out of Matter, which itself prepares? All the Difference is, the doing that in an Instant which the Creature must take Time to do. For, as for the Preparation of Matter, that must be made fit, be the Agent never so omnipotent."

19. *Ibid.,* 48–49.

20. *Ibid.,* 58–59: "But notwithstanding all I have said, in Defence of the Creation of the Individuals of all Animals at first, because the inconceivable smallness of the last Races of Animals make it incredible, I shall content to let it pass for a Conjecture, and not insist further on it." Rádl (132) writes: "Ray, who . . . believed in preformation"—what truth there is in this claim is clear from the passage just cited. We will have further occasion to return to Rádl's work, which enjoys a rather undeserved high reputation.

seems fully certain of is that the parent animals have nothing to do
with procreation since *generatio* is "a work of art and reason" beyond the ability of animals; man, too, does not understand the process of procreation within himself, and since he is not aware of the
processes taking place inside him, he clearly cannot be the agent
causing them.[21]

21. Ray, *Three Physico-Theological Discourses*, 48–49: "Nor, indeed, doth Man
himself understand anything of the Process of Generation in himself, neither is conscious of what is done in the Womb; so far is he from being the Doer of it."

2

Man's Position in the System of Nature

We were able to show what the problem of biological species looked like in the eighteenth century by presenting the theories of Linnaeus and Ray and their ramifications in the views Kant and Goethe had of the living form; thus, the full scope of the problem's speculative possibilities became evident. The dominant idea was the fixity of the species, and from this developed the notion of a nature "in itself" and, in contrast to the classification systems, the idea of a real-ontological division of life forms by which scientific description must be guided. This idea of nature brought with it the question of the "natural" criterion by which to differentiate the subdivisions as opposed to the logical-specific one. This question is answered, on the one hand, by the thesis of the unity of descent and of the species-wide capacity to interbreed as the natural *cause* of the species unity and, on the other hand, by reference to the essence of the species that can be intuitively perceived in the individual and that must guide the conceptual formulation of the essential type. And finally, the genetic question cannot be ignored, a question Ray still left undecided, namely, whether each individual is created by a direct act of God or whether the one-time creation of the species with a complicated mechanism for the unfolding of all the seeds contained in the first individual over the course of generations was sufficient. We still have to trace all these beginnings through their development; now we consider how man was incorporated into this early natural system.

The first great nature systems, those of Buffon and Linnaeus, comprise the whole of nature in all its forms, taking man as one of these forms. Buffon formulated the problem connected with this ordering more clearly than did Linnaeus, and we will therefore analyze his idea first, although his system is chronologically later.

§1. Buffon

In his doctrine of man, Buffon was a Cartesian. Following the position of the Cartesian *Meditation,* he speaks of a *sens intérieur* that enables us to recognize our innermost being and to free it from all illusions our external activity evokes in us about the world and ourselves. The result of the reflection of the internal sense is the realization that there are two substances, soul and matter. The one is not extensive and immortal, the other is extensive and passes away. We know for sure that the soul exists, but we may have doubts about the existence of matter. The substance of the soul is simple and indivisible and has only one modification: thinking. Matter is multifarious, divisible, and can assume a variety of forms. Being and thinking are one and the same for us—this insight, according to Buffon, is immediate and independent of our senses, our imagination, or our memory. The existence of one's body, on the other hand, and that of the other external objects remains doubtful to anyone thinking without prejudices.[1] Buffon coarsens and absolutizes the method of the Cartesian *Meditation,* in which the reality of the world is doubted in order to gain the secure point from which its existence finally appears as certain. Descartes' "suspended" judgment on existence is turned into an absolutely doubtful one, and the doubtful existence of the mind in its duration, for which Descartes required a special procedure of proof, is posited as unconditionally certain. The Cartesian dualism is thus intensified, and this deepening of the chasm prepares the way for the possibility of treating man as part of natural history in regard to his body without the connection to the soul, that is, without the body-soul unity of man becoming a problem. The soul, according to Buffon, is completely different from and of an infinitely higher order than matter.[2] Man's soul is his essence,

---

1. Buffon, *Histoire naturelle générale et particulière* (1749), Pt. 4, p. 155: "Etre et penser, sont pour nous la même chose, cette vérité est intime et plus qu'intuitive, elle est indépendante de nos sens, de notre imagination, de notre mémoire et de toutes nos autres facultés relatives. . . . L'existence de notre corps et des autres objets extérieurs est douteuse pour quiconque raisonne sans préjugé." [To exist and to think for us are the same thing—this truth is intimate and more than intuitive, it is independent of our senses, of our imagination, of our memory, and of all our other related faculties. . . . The existence of our body and of other external objects is doubtful for anyone who reasons without prejudice.]

2. *Ibid.,* 159: The soul is "d'une nature totalement différente, et d'un ordre infiniment supérieur" [of a totally different nature, and of an infinitely superior order].

and that is why man as a whole can be said to be completely different in his essence from the animals and to resemble them only outwardly.[3] According to the construction type of differential concepts,[4] the soul is declared to be the human essence in the true sense: the inner man is the true man, the external one is only an animalistic mechanism with a bodily soul, an animated cadaver that has nothing to do with the human essence. A clean cut separates the lower animal half from the upper human half so completely that the question of how these two halves are nevertheless the halves of one whole appears absurd. The passage can close calmly with the pronouncement that the spirituality of the inner man having been proven, the outer man can now be studied in the history of his body.[5]

This clear line of construction, however, is interrupted by objections Buffon can allay only through reflections on methodology. The body-soul unity of man cannot, after all, be completely ignored, and in spite of the complete separation of soul and matter, integrating man into the natural system is inevitably accompanied by the uncomfortable feeling that man is thus placed on a level with the animals. To squelch this feeling, Buffon engages in a brief digression on the method of classification; this passage has received a great deal of attention and has frequently been cited as expressing a definitive opinion of the author. Though we cannot agree that it is definitive (since Buffon worked the problem out with meticulous thoroughness elsewhere), it is nevertheless characteristic of the speculative situation, for here Buffon admits that he has placed man on a level with the animals, but to tone down this admission, he considers this leveling merely a convention without real-ontological significance. Nature, he argues, knows no classes and genera, but only individuals. The groups we form are the work of our mind; they are conventional ideas, and classifying man as belonging to one of these

---

3. *Ibid.*, 172: "Il est évident que l'homme est d'une nature entièrement différente de celle de l'animal, qu'il ne lui ressemble que par l'extérieur." [It is evident that man is of an entirely different nature from that of the animal, that he is in no way similar to it, except externally.]

4. See the Introduction, §2, and my *Race and State*, the chapter entitled "Body-Soul-Spirit."

5. Buffon, *Histoire naturelle*, 172: "Après avoir considéré l'homme intérieur, et avoir démontré la spiritualité de son âme, nous pouvons maintenant examiner l'homme extérieur, et faire l'histoire de son corps." [After having considered the interior man, and having demonstrated the spirituality of his soul, we can now examine the external man, and treat the history of his body.]

46

groups does not alter his real status in any way; it means no more than putting him in one group with the objects he most resembles materially.[6]

This conventionalist digression contains so many internal contradictions that for this reason alone we cannot regard it as a well-considered, definitive opinion. For even if we assume that Buffon uses the terms *classe* and *genre* in a precise sense and consciously avoids the term *espèce* (so that conventional unity could indeed be conceded to classes and genera, the species remain without doubt as ontic-real divisions), this conventionalism surely cannot extend to the ontic realms of plants, animals, and man, whose distinct essences as created by God Buffon has never doubted. At any rate, conventionalism in Buffon's system cannot go so far as to ignore the real differences between man and the animals and to include man among the animals.

This passage is therefore immediately followed by a very insistent listing of all the predispositions and faculties that distinguish man from the animals: pragmatic intelligence, the ability to make plans, the creation of signs for processes of the soul's life, language, thought, insights, invention, the predisposition to perfection.[7] Indeed, the efforts to distinguish man from the animals go so far as to consider the transition from man to animal an exception to the rule that nature is not discontinuous. According to Buffon, there are no connecting links between man and animal; instead there is a discontinuity between the thinking being and the pure mechanism, such as is found even in the highest animal species, the apes.[8] The benev-

---

6. *Ibid.*, 162–63: "Mais, comme je l'ai déjà fait sentir, la Nature n'a ni classes ni genres, elle ne comprend que des individus; ces genres et ces classes sont l'ouvrage de notre esprit, ce ne sont que des idées de convention, et lorsque nous mettons l'homme dans l'une de ces classes, nous ne changeons pas la réalité de son être, nous ne dérogeons point à sa noblesse, nous n'altérons pas sa condition, enfin nous n'ôtons n'en à la supériorité de la nature humaine sur celles des brutes, nous ne faisons que placer l'homme avec ce qui lui ressemble le plus, en donnant même à la partie matérielle de son être le premier rang." [But, as I have already indicated, nature has neither classes nor genera, it consists in nothing but individuals; these genera and classes are the work of our mind, they are nothing but conventional ideas, and when we place man in one of these classes, we do not change the reality of his being, we do not go against his nobility, we do not debase him to the level of the brutes, we do nothing but place man with that which resembles him most, even in bestowing the first rank on the material part of his being.]

7. *Ibid.*, 164–65.

8. *Ibid.*, 170–71: Cette vérité qui d'ailleurs ne souffre aucune exception, se dément ici tout à fait; il y a une distance infinie entre les facultés de l'homme et celles du plus parfait animal, preuve évidente que l'homme est d'une différente nature, que

Only similarities betw. humans + animals are external.

olence of the creator has placed a *distance immense* between man and animal, limiting any similarities to externals.[9] This speculative schema compels Buffon to ambiguous claims, according to which man, because of his integration into the natural system, is actually classified as belonging to a supposedly real natural order. But since this classification necessarily applies only to one part of the whole human being, it conflicts with the idea of the human being as a unified whole. Therefore, the natural order must be presented as a conventionalist one that has no significance at all for the real status of the objects subsumed under the same order. However, the conventionalism is done away with again by the thesis that the two substances soul and mechanical matter are *in reality* separated by an immense chasm through divine ordinance.

The separation of man and animal, then, is real and not mere convention. Man can be integrated into the system of nature only if his material and spiritual parts are separated, which is made emotionally easier through the rationalist concept of the human person. We have just seen the details of the structure of the person in his pragmatic faculties, the rational system of signs, and progress toward perfection, and the same conceptual orientation also shapes the total image of the person that became so important for the rationalist democratic idea in the eighteenth century. Above all, the person is here conceived of only in its adult manifestation, and the entire maturation of man as a bodily-spiritual being is excluded as unimportant. "Un homme doit regarder comme nulles les 15 premières

---

seul il fait une classe à part de laquelle il faut descendre en parcourant un espace infini avant que d'arriver à celle des animaux; car si l'homme était de l'ordre des animaux, il y aurait dans la Nature un certain nombre d'êtres moins parfaits que l'homme et plus parfaits que l'animal, par lesquelles on descendroit insensiblement et par nuances de l'homme au singe; mais cela n'est pas, on passe tout d'un coup de l'être pensant à l'être matériel, de la puissance intellectuelle à la force méchanique, de l'ordre et du dessein au mouvement aveugle, de la réflexion à l'appétit.

[This truth that otherwise does not suffer any exception, is completely refuted here; that there is an infinite distance between the faculties of man and those of the most perfect animal evidently proves that man is of a different nature, that only he makes a class departing from which one must descend through an infinite space before arriving at that of the animals; for if man were of the order of the animals there would be in nature a certain number of beings less perfect than man and more perfect than the animal through which one descends insensibly and by way of nuances from man to the monkey; but that does not occur, one passes all at once from the thinking being to the material being, from the intellectual power to mechanical force, from order and design to blind movement, from reflection to appetite.]

9. *Ibid.*, 171–72.

années de sa vie." [A person should completely disregard the first fifteen years of his or her life.] Everything that happens to people in the course of those years, Buffon argues, is erased from their memory or is so little connected to what concerns them later that it is of no interest at all to them. Aging as the basic process of the person, as we think of it today, was still inconceivable back then; the person does not *become*, it does not mature throughout life until the moment of death; it simply *is*, beginning with a particular moment that is reached with puberty, and it remains unalterably the same until its death.

It is highly characteristic that these reflections of Buffon are found in the chapter on age and death and are intended as consolation for the pathetic impression the extensive mortality statistics make on the reader. From these it is clear that at the age of twenty-eight or twenty-nine, one half of life is over; to repel this thought Buffon points out that the first fifteen years should not be counted and the middle of life would then not be reached until about age thirty-six. The thought that all life is a living toward death and only has meaning in this view is to be pushed away if at all possible. The life of the adult is to be completely separated from the life of the growing and developing person, as completely, in fact, as the soul is separated from the body. Adult life does not belong to the same stream of ideas as the maturing life; we do not begin to live in the spiritual sense until we begin to order our own thoughts, to direct them toward a definite goal in the future, that is, we do not live until we begin to take a firm stance in regard to our aim in life.[10] The person is not real until he or she has attained a rational mainstay of habits and arrangements geared to a definite goal, that is, until everyday life has found its fixed, regulated course, from which it does not dream to deviate. This is a thoroughly bourgeois-stable idea, for which social status and profession are the lasting and regulating forms of life. This isolation of life's rational regular-

---

10. *Ibid.*, 424: "Ce n'est pas la même succession d'idées, ni, pour ainsi dire, la même vie; nous ne commençons à vivre moralement que quand nous commençons à ordonner nos pensées, à les tourner vers un certain avenir, et à prendre une espèce de consistance, un état relatif à ce que nous devons être dans la suite." [This is not the same succession of ideas, nor, so to speak, the same life; we do not begin to live morally until we start to order our thoughts, to turn them toward a certain future, and to take hold of a kind of consistency, a condition related to what we ought to be in the future.]

ity favors particularly the separation of the body as something external to man and its discussion under the heading of the animal kingdom.

Buffon's theory belongs to the isolating constructions, to the type of constructions that isolate the essence from the entity as a whole. For our study of the speculative schemata this theory is extraordinarily instructive because it shows that in spite of the complete and total splitting of the human essence into its parts, the subhuman body and the truly human soul, the experience of the unity formed by these parts is strong enough to require the strange conventionalistic secondary constructions we have just encountered. Buffon's theory is of decisive significance for the historical development of the race idea because here the theoretical defects that still beset race theory today appear for the first time in a thoroughly rationalized and therefore clearly visible form. That man is a body-soul unity can no more be denied than the possibility of studying the body in isolation and with scientific methods. But how these two facts can be reconciled and how the essence of man can be determined remain unresolved questions. Although Buffon isolated the material element of man, he did not come to the obvious conclusion in his dualistic philosophy and limit his typology of races to physical traits only. Rather, as we shall see below, he cites both physical and spiritual traits and also includes in his descriptions comments on manners and customs, religious notions, the state of civilization, governmental forms, and the like. This compilation of data still falls short of a thought-out system; instead the facts are cited based on their value as curiosities, but the external form is already the same one we see in modern works on race theory.

§2. Linnaeus

In Linnaeus' work we find the same confusion as in Buffon's, but in Linnaeus it takes more naive forms since this intuitive yet effusively pious man did not rack his brain excessively about theoretical questions. We must present the basic features of his classification of man since his description of *Homo europaeus* has become the model for the subsequent typology of Nordic man—Georges Vacher de Lapouge cites the Linnaean system, as does Hans Günther.[11] Linnaeus makes no attempt to justify his inclusion of man in his system of nature, he simply classifies man with the animals and at the same time expatiates in rapturous exclamations on the superior dignity of man. "Inter omnia, numquam satis praedicanda, Orbis Terraquei Miracula, ipso Homine, nihil omnino illustrius, potius nihil est." [That there is nothing more illustrious among all the world's marvels, indeed simply nothing, than man himself can never be proclaimed enough.] But man nevertheless belongs among the *quadrupedia*, in fact, because he is not a stone, plant, worm, insect, fish, or fowl—he therefore cannot be anything but four-footed, and the naturalists' comparative researches show that no specific bodily features can be found that distinguish man from the apes. The higher rank of man, Linnaeus argues, is due to a characteristic that cannot be perceived by the senses, namely, reason. This invisible trait, justifying his superiority, is the pledge of man's divine origin.[12]

However much man as ruler over the dead and the living world is elevated above all other kingdoms of nature, he nevertheless belongs to the totality of creation, and Linnaeus apparently did not find the classification of man with the animals in any way embar-

11. Georges Vacher de Lapouge, *Les Sélections sociales* (Paris, 1896), 13, 171. Hans F. K. Günther, *Rassenkunde des deutschen Volkes*, 15th ed. (Munich, 1930), 16, 205. See also Houston Stewart Chamberlain, *Arische Weltanschauung* (Munich, 1916), 11.

12. Presentation in *Linnaei Fauna Suecica: Editio altera. Auctior* (Stockholm, 1761; 1st ed. 1746), "Praefatio." The Preface is not paginated; it amounts to nine pages in all. Concerning language as a distinguishing trait: "Loquela quidem Hominem a reliquis animalibus distinguere videtur, verum enim vero haec quaedam est potentia vel certe effectus, non autem nota characteristica a numero, figura, proportione aut situ desumpta; ut res adeo sit, per quam arduae indaginis, propriam tradere hominis differentiam specificam." [Speech indeed seems to distinguish man from the rest of the animals; yet nevertheless this is a determinate potency or surely an effect but not a characteristic mark drawn from number, shape, proportion, or location; so that it is still a thing, through which arduous investigation renders the proper specific difference of man.]

On reason: "Ast in nobis quidquam inest, quod visum non subit, unde nostri ipsorum cognitio pendet, utpote nobilissima *Ratio*, qua Homo cunctis animalibus immane quantum praecellit. . . . Itaque omnium, quos produxit Deus, universi orbis incolarum, hoc est, omnium animalium praestantissimus est homo, cui proinde, singulari verique paterno moderamine, praeesse, et quam optime prospicere voluit Beneficentissimus ille Naturae Auctor." [But in us there is something not susceptible of being seen, whence our knowledge of ourselves depends, that is to say, the most noble *reason*, by which man stands out vastly above all animals. . . . Therefore, of all the inhabitants of the entire world, which God has produced, that is to say, ahead of all the animals stands man, over whom therefore a singular and truly paternal governor rules and upon whom that most beneficent Author of nature deigned to look.]

yes!

rassing or disturbing. Man and the rest of the world are so close to each other, because they are all part of God's creation, that the classifications have no decisive significance. All species of creatures were included in the great unity of Paradise, and man's relationship to the plants and animals was not one of active subjugation and domination but one of careful, ordering examination. Paradise was the first botanical garden, and man's tasks were: *Inspectio Creaturarum, et Impositio Nominum. Zoologiae studium* was the first concern of man in his happiest state, and the study of nature has remained his task even after the expulsion from Paradise, insofar as the cares of everyday life leave him time for this pursuit. The *Horti Botanici* are the *minores Paradisi.* The breath of God wafts through the entire world, making one part the delight and pleasure of the other—without man's having to worry anxiously about his own rank, which, like that of all other creatures, was conferred by God.[13]

Man and his subspecies are presented as intimately connected with the other primates. The first *classis* introduced is that of Mammalia; the first *ordo* under it is the primates; and the first of the *characteres* of the primates is *Homo. Homo* is followed by *Simia, Lemur,* and *Vespertilio* as belonging to the same *ordo,* resulting in the following table of characters, with the added *differentiis specificis:*

1. *Homo: Nosce te ipsum.*
2. *Simia: Dentes laniarii.*
3. *Lemur: Dentes primores inferiores 6.*
4. *Vespertilio: Manus palmato-volatiles.*

Thus the *dentes laniarii* and others were placed on the same level as *nosce te ipsum* in a series of distinguishing characteristics. That these characteristics belong to different spheres of being is not taken

---

13. Linnaeus, *Fauna Suecica,* "Praefatio": "Animali huic formosissimo, ut omnium sapientissimo, ita constituto orbis terrarum Regi et Domino, splendidissimam sedem suapte manu paratam, Deus attribuit, Paradisum loquor sive Hortum Eden, maxima omnium eorum, queis opus erat, affluentia spectabilem. Heic omnia Animalia, Plantae omnes fuere; adeoque maxime varietas, maxime voluptas. Ecce, primum vereque primarium *Hortum Botanicum* . . . ; Ecce primas hominis curas, delicias primas, *Animalia et Plantas.*" [God gave to this most beautiful of animals, as wisest of all, and so constituted to be King and Lord of the earth, a most splendid site so fittingly prepared by his hand, I say that paradise or the Garden of Eden was remarkable for the greatest abundance of everything that was needed. Here were every animal, every plant, and the greatest variety besides, the supreme pleasure. Behold, the first and truly original *Botanical Garden.* . . . Behold the first of man's cares, the first delights, *animals and plants.*]

into consideration, and the further typology of the subspecies also reveals the same mixture of physical, characterological, and institutional elements as Buffon's typology. Linnaeus, however, followed a certain order in his description and formed the classes of traits that have served as the model for subsequent theoreticians down to the present day. Linnaeus distinguishes (aside from the "wild" and monstrous types) among American, European, Asian, and African people; of these, the type *Homo europaeus* is especially important for us. The first traits listed are skin color, temperament (in the physiological sense), and body type (*albus, sanguineus, torosus*); hair and eye color follow (*pilis flavescentibus prolixis, oculis coeruleis*), then traits of soul (*levis, argutus, inventor*), and further the type of body covering (*tegitur vestimentis arctis*) and finally the type of habitual regularity [*Regelhaftigkeit*] of the spirit (*regitur ritibus*).[14] The other subspecies are described according to the state of knowledge at the time.[15]

---

14. Linnaeus, *Systema Naturae*, 13th ed. (Vienna, 1767; 1st ed., 1735), 19, 24, 29. The first editions do not yet include the racial types. The size of the work increases considerably from edition to edition. The earliest available to me, the second edition of 1740, consists of eighty octavo pages; the thirteenth fills four thick volumes.

15. A classification of the racial types found in Sweden is contained in *Fauna Suecica* (2d ed., 1761). Here, too, man is listed as the first animal species, under the title of *Homo sapiens* (a word combination that already implies the soul-body duality); the *differentia specifica* given here is not *Nosce te ipsum* [know thyself] but *Naturae regnorum tyrannus* [tyrant of the realms of nature], thus designating less the spiritual essence itself than the deep contrast between man and subhuman nature. The subspecies listed here are the Sveci, Gothi, Fennones, and Lappones. The description is somewhat clearer in that only physical traits are used for characterizations; for the Gothi (who correspond to the *Homo Europaeus* of the other work) they are: *Corpore proceriore, Capillis albidis, Oculorum iridibus cinereo-caerulescentibus*. It is not until the notes on the four types that habitations, origin, and, in one case, ways of life and housing are mentioned (p. 1).

3

Travelogues

The choice of Linnaeus' and Buffon's systems as the point of departure for our analysis of the historical constitution of the race idea
was not as arbitrary as it might seem when we consider only the
problems of their systems we have discussed in the preceding chapter. We are now familiar with the structure of the biological problem
of species around the middle of the eighteenth century, and we are
familiar with the position of man in the order of living beings and
understand which constructions made it possible to include man in
a descriptive system of nature. Of course, there were descriptions of
the plant and animal world several decades earlier—I refer only to
the work of Ray and Willughby—and the question of man's position
in the world is a topic that was part of every metaphysical essay, and
Buffon's variation of it is, moreover, simply a recapitulation of Descartes' ideas. That the problem of the nature of man at that time developed into an ordering of the physical diversity of humanity and
thus became connected with the classification of nature is due to a
particular historical factor, namely, the expansion of the geographic
horizon, of the knowledge of man, through the growing wealth of
material provided by travelogues ever since the Renaissance. Kant
refers to these travelogues, remarking that they were the incentive
for the study of the physical diversity of man.[1]

Over the centuries knowledge of man and his distribution over
the earth grew, and by the middle of the eighteenth century, it was
ready to be compiled in large-scale syntheses. The systems of Linnaeus and Buffon present for the first time all the knowledge available at that time about living nature and man. Buffon's system in
particular became representative for the understanding of nature of

1. Kant, *Bestimmung des Begriffs einer Menschenrace* (Philosophische Bibliothek, 1785), 125. "The information the new travels offer about the diversity of the human race has so far tended more to stimulate the mind to further research on this
point than to satisfy it."

that era and for the advances of human achievement in attaining it; this system became the medium through which that expansion of the geographical horizon was brought home to the educated public. In a note written in March of 1832 Goethe mentions that his life was early on touched undefinably but strongly by an echo of natural history, because Buffon had published the first part of the *Histoire naturelle* in the year of Goethe's birth and subsequent volumes followed each year. This publication aroused great interest among the Germans, who at the time were very open to French influence, "and thus the interests of an educated community accompanied my growing years."[2]

Neither Linnaeus nor Buffon arranged the various diverse human types in a self-contained system; both presented them merely as one part of the great diversity of natural phenomena in general, on a par with minerals, plants, and animals. That is why we find such peculiar connections between the discussion of man and the other classes of natural phenomena. Linnaeus weaves a succinct typology of human races into his *Systema Naturae*, and it also appears in his work on the Swedish fauna. In Buffon's work the study of man forms a part of the above-mentioned *Histoire naturelle, générale, et particulière.*

The attempt to arrange the types systematically into a unified order could be successfully undertaken because—as we have said—the geographic horizon of information about distant peoples had broadened to an extraordinary extent. Buffon's work, which provides a wealth of source references, gives us a glimpse of the large amount of material available at that time. The chapter entitled "Variétés dans l' espèce humaine," in the sixth volume of the *Histoire*, cites more than eighty titles of travel books, collections of travel writings, and accounts of European and non-European peoples.[3] There is little use in listing all of them here simply to give the impressive effect of the sheer number of sources, but we want to print out a few titles to give a general idea of the depth and breadth of the material in its history, content, and origin.

2. Goethe, "Zur Naturwissenschaft im allgemeinen," in *Principes de Philosophie Zoologique par Geoffroy de Saint-Hilaire,* Vol. XXXVI of *Goethes Werke* (Cotta, 1827–42), 308.

3. Buffon, *Histoire naturelle, générale et particulière, Avec la description du Cabinet du Roy,* 4th ed. (1752) VI, 98–335.

The oldest travel report Buffon uses is that of Marco Polo dating from the thirteenth century. The sixteenth century saw the travels of Pigafetta, the observations of Pierre Belon, and Jean de Lery's voyage to Brazil; Buffon mentions Pigafetta's *India Orientalis*, emphasizing particularly the voyage of Jean Hugon described in the second volume, and he also refers to Belon's observations on Turkey. There is a notable increase of available material from the seventeenth century: Buffon cites the *Genio vagante del conte Aurelio degli Anzi*; the voyages of Pyrard, Thévenot, and Villamont; an anonymous *Nouvelle relation du Levant* of 1667; a Spanish book of travels; *Olaii Rudbekii Atlantica*; a *Relation curieuse de Moscovie*, the report from one of Emperor Leopold's emissaries to the czar; a collection of *Voyages historique de l'Europe*; a history of the Antilles by a missionary; a book of travels among the Hurons; the *Histoire de la conquéte de la Chine par les Tartars* by Palafox; the travel works of Johann Albrecht von Mandelslo (Persia, East India, Madagascar); the history of the first discovery of the Canary Islands by Bontier and Jean le Verrier; and many more. But the vast majority of the sources dates from the first half of the eighteenth century, especially the great collections: *Recueil des voyages, qui ont servi à l'établissement et au progrès de la compagnie des Indes orientales, formée dans les Provinces-unies des Pais-Bas; Recueil des voyages au Nord, contenant divers Memoires très utiles au commerce et à la navigation;* and finally the *Lettres édifiantes et curieuses, écrites des missions étrangères, par quelques missionaires de la compagnie de Jésus,* the first volume of which appeared in 1703. In addition, there are (selected from among many others): the frequently cited travels of Jean Struys, Le Gentil, Chardin, and Ovington; the *Histoire générale des voyages* of 1746; a description of the island of Formosa; a history of the Marianas, of the conquest of the Moluccas, and of Ceylon; Bosman's voyage to Guinea; a history of San Domingo; a description of the Cape of Good Hope, of New France; a voyage to the Amazon area; and a history of the Incas.

4

The Classification of Races: Buffon

The first great systems for classifying human races were based on the material presented in the travel writings. The way these systems treat the material is of crucial importance for the development of the race idea because here the foundation is laid for the classification still in use today—vacillating between establishing biological divisions in the strict sense and collectives [*Kollektiva*] identified by their historical and geographical distribution. While the identification of these collective entities is nowadays typically overlaid by theories claiming that they are also exact biological units, in its beginnings classification is still relatively free from biologizing reinterpretations and therefore allows us to recognize more clearly the actual criteria for the definition of the groups. Buffon's race divisions are especially instructive in this regard because he does not yet differentiate between the significance of physical and spiritual traits, and the concept *race* is not yet firmly defined and delimited. That is why we will consider his race classification first.

§1. *Espèce* and *variété*

As mentioned above, Buffon treats the *espèce humaine* and its *variété* in his discussion of the animals though he grants it a special rank in the animal kingdom because of its *noblesse*. Nevertheless, according to Buffon, man resembles the animals in his physical aspect, and if he is to be included in the list of all living beings, he must therefore be placed into one class with the animals.[1] However, he does not rigidly maintain this classification, for in his actual descriptions of the human varieties Buffon does not limit his list of characteristics to the physical and outer ones, which were the rea-

---

1. Buffon, *Histoire naturelle*, Pt. 4, pp. 126ff.

*physical &
spiritual traits
listed together as a
unified
whole*

son for including man in the animal kingdom in the first place. Instead, Buffon also lists characterological and institutional peculiarities of the peoples and races under discussion. Buffon's major considerations in his descriptions are skin color, physique, and height, and finally the "disposition" of the various tribes.[2] The physical and spiritual traits are listed together as though they belonged to the same realm of being; man is seen as a unified whole exhibiting the various traits. The question of the causal relationship between physical and spiritual traits, so central to the race theory of the late nineteenth century, does not yet come up. Buffon nowhere attempts to establish a causal relationship between somatic elements and specific character traits; on the contrary, at times he allows himself to speak of a racial difference in spite of somatic kinship when the customs of the tribes under discussion differ widely from each other. In Buffon's work the boundary between physical and spiritual traits is still fluid and flexible, and both serve equally to characterize exotic human types.

§2. The Norm and the Exotic

The exoticism of some varieties in contrast to the familiar European type that was taken as the norm is the central idea in Buffon's description. According to him, the white European represents the purest realization of the idea of man in body, soul, and spirit, and the numerous varieties that have become known through travel writings are accordingly seen as deviations from the norm that is never questioned as such. Just as the accumulation of material expanded the knowledge of man in the geographical dimension, so the description aims at an arrangement of types covering a large area, based on the criterion of distance from the normal type and eschewing the depth dimension of history. An example will illustrate this kind of description: The study begins with a description of Laplanders; they are described as "une race d'hommes de petite stature, d'une figure

2. Buffon, *Histoire naturelle*, Pt. 6, p. 98: "La première et la plus remarquable de ces variétés est celle de la couleur, la seconde est celle de la forme et de la grandeur, et la troisième est celle du naturel des différens peuples." [The first and most remarkable of these varieties is that of color, the second is that of shape and size, and the third is that of what comes naturally to different peoples.]

bizarre, dont la physiognomie est aussi sauvage que les moeurs" [a race of men of small stature, with a strange (*bizarre*) shape, whose physiognomy is as wild (*sauvage*) as their customs]. *Bizarre* and *sauvage* are judgmental epithets, intended to show the readers clearly that this breed of men deviates significantly from the familiar ideals of beauty. The derogatory impression is underlined by the claim that these people "paraissent avoir dégénéré de l'espèce humaine" [appear to have degenerated from the human species]. The damning judgment is then generalized to the entire group of related peoples—to Danish, Swedish, and Russian Lapps, to Samoyeds, Tatars, Ostyaks, Greenlanders, and Eskimos. "Non seulement ces peuples se ressemblent par la laideur, la petitesse de la taille, la couleur des cheveux et des yeux, mais ils ont aussi tous à peu près les mêmes inclinations et les mêmes moeurs" [Not only do these peoples resemble each other in virtue of their ugliness, the smallness of their size, the color of their hair and eyes, but they also have nearly the same inclinations and mores]—they are all equally "coarse, superstitious, stupid."[3] This is followed by detailed descriptions of their religious customs, family and sexual mores, their way of life, diet, dwellings, and clothing. Buffon stresses in particular that they have no religion to speak of since they are lacking the idea of a highest being, that they are rough and common rather than wild, that they lack all self-respect, and that this *peuple abject* is only just civilized enough to merit contempt. Buffon was especially horrified at their habit of bathing together in the nude, boys and girls, mothers and sons, brothers and sisters, without being in the least ashamed in front of each other. But the most horrible by far was that "en sortant de ces bains extrêmement chauds, ils vont se jeter dans une rivière très froide" [leaving their extremely hot baths, they usually throw themselves into a very chilly river].[4] The Laplanders offer their wives to strangers who come among them, and in Buffon's opinion this is because they are aware that their women are misshapen and ugly—and "ils trouvent apparemment moins laides celles que les étrangers n'ont pas dédaignées" [and they apparently find less ugly those whom the strangers have not scorned].[5]

3. *Ibid.*, 102.
4. *Ibid.*, 104.
5. *Ibid.*, 107.

§3. Race

The exotic types are deviations from a norm; exploring the globe reveals numerous colorful varieties, and the various groups of traits and the terms to designate them are still fluid and have not yet become firmly defined and unequivocal. The discussion of races is still vague, lacking that strict sense of the bodily type and the soul type causally connected to it that is characteristic of race theory in the nineteenth century. The Laplanders are considered a race, the *race Lapponne*, though beyond the anecdotal description of physical traits, morals, and customs, no specific criteria are given for regarding these tribes as a unified entity. Buffon indulges in the sort of colorful description that today we would be inclined to call ethnography or ethnology rather than anthropology or race theory. After the Laplanders, the Tatars are presented at equal length and with as much detail, and the *race Tartare* is put on a par with the *race Lapponne*; subdivisions within these "races" are called *différences particulières*. That the element of common descent plays a part—though not a clearly defined one—in this notion of race can be seen here and there in some of Buffon's comments. For example, he claims that the "nation" of the Muscovites is "of the same blood as the other European nations." The European race appears here as sharing the same blood, a unit that can be divided into the ethnic subgroups of nations. But since the idea of blood is not yet fixed and the shared blood cannot be unequivocally correlated to characterological types, the conflict between somatic and social traits can lead to doubts about the division into races. The Chinese, for example, are physically not so different from the Tatars that Buffon would have to designate them a separate race for that reason. According to Buffon, the only reason that might justify such a subdivision is the strong difference in morals and customs between the two peoples.[6]

In another case, however, cultural similarity seems sufficiently strong to outweigh all somatic differences—for example, Buffon claims that the Ethiopians are of white origin, "puisqu'ils ont la

---

6. *Ibid.*, 212: "La seule chose qui pourrait le faire croire, c'est la différence totale du naturel, des moeurs et des coutumes de ces deux peuples." [The only thing that can make us believe this is the total difference in what comes naturally, in the manners and customs of the two peoples.]

For Buffon, customs + morals differentiates peoples just as much as physical traits

même religion et les mêmes usages que les Arabes" [since they have the same religion and the same customs as the Arabs].[7] The vacillation in the terminology is particularly clear in Buffon's description of the African tribes; on the one hand he talks of a "description des *peuples* de l'Afrique" [description of the *peuples* of Africa], of the "*nations* de toute la partie septentrionale de l'Afrique" [the *nations* of the northern part of Africa], and of the "*espèces* de Maures" [*species* of Moors] who settled the terrain from the Red Sea to the ocean.[8] A few pages later, a single sentence overturns the distinction between a European race on the one hand and the *race Lapponne, race Tartare,* and so forth, on the other and instead speaks of the black and white races and their subdivisions. The black and white races, Buffon here maintains, are the supreme groups and can be subdivided into similar varieties. Thus, the black race has its Tatars and Circassians just as the white race does, and furthermore, these subunits are also called "races."[9] A few lines later, the two races, Negroes and Kaffirs, are again called "ces deux espèces d'hommes noirs" [the two species of black men]; that is, the same concept of species is applied to them that in other contexts serves to designate all of mankind as an animal species. The concept of variety, usually used to designate groups like the Circassians, Kaffirs, Tatars, and others, is also used in the subdivision of these groups into smaller units, and finally, *nuance* serves as a synonym to designate these smallest units.[10]

§4. Causes of Differences Among the Races

The description of races seems more loose than it really is because Buffon proceeds from one geographic area to the adjacent one in his

7. *Ibid.,* 263.
8. *Ibid.,* 212.
9. *Ibid.,* 219: "Il paraît . . . qu'il y a autant de variété dans la race des noirs, que dans celle des blancs; les noirs ont, comme les blancs, leurs Tartares et leurs Circassiens. . . . Il est donc nécessaire de diviser les noirs en différentes races, et il me semble qu'on peut les réduire à deux principales, celle des Nègres et celles des Caffres." [It appears . . . that there is as much variety in the black race as in that of the whites; the blacks have their Tartars and their Circassians. . . . It is therefore necessary to divide the blacks into different races, and it seems to me that one can reduce them to two principal ones, that of the Negroes and that of the Kaffirs.]
10. *Ibid.,* 221: "Ensuite en examinant en particulier les différents peuples qui composent chacune de ces races noires, nous y verrons autant de variétés que dans les races blanches, et nous y trouverons les nuances du brun au noir, comme nous avon trouvé dans les races blanches toutes les nuances du brun au blanc." [Later on in examining in particular the different peoples that make up each of the black races, we

discussion. In fact, however, each race is judged according to how close it comes to the norm, and the deviation from the norm is put down to specific causative factors. For Buffon three types of causes suffice to explain all observable differences: climate, diet, and customs.[11] In practical terms, customs play a very minor role in Buffon's classification of variations, which is probably due to the methodological difficulty of determining without a doubt whether the customs are cause or effect in a particular case. To diet as a determining cause Buffon refers only in passing. As he explains, differences in diet affect mostly the body form and shapeliness [*Wohlgestalt*]; this leads Buffon to comment on the difference between undernourished peasants and well-fed city dwellers.[12]

In Buffon's method, the most important causal factor is climate because it is responsible for the differences in the most obvious distinguishing feature, skin color: "On peut donc regarder le climat comme la cause première et presque unique de la couleur des hommes." [Thus one can consider climate as the primary and almost unique cause of man's color.][13] The color divisions are based on the distance from the equator. The belt between twenty and thirty or thirty-five degrees north latitude stretches from the Ganges to the western coast of Morocco and is settled by a unified type: "Les hommes en général y sont brun et basané, mais ils sont au même temps assez beaux et assez bien faits." [In general the people there are brown and tan, but at the same time they are quite handsome and good-looking.][14] To the north of this area there is a temperate zone, settled by Armenians, Turks, Georgians, Mingrelians, Circassians, Greeks, and the European peoples; these men are "les plus beaux, les plus blancs et les mieux faits de toute la terre" [the most beautiful, the whitest, and the best-looking in the world].[15] Because of the hotter climate, the people living in the southern part of this zone are browner; the zone extends northward all the way to Lapland, where "une autre espèce d'hommes" [another species of man] lives, for the dry cold has a similar coloring effect on the normal human complex-

note as many varieties as in the white races, and we find the nuances from brown to black, just as we have found all the nuances from brown to white in the white races.]

11. *Ibid.*, 212.
12. *Ibid.*, 332.
13. *Ibid.*, 331–32.
14. *Ibid.*, 190.
15. *Ibid.*

ion as does heat.[16] The Negro peoples exhibit a similar gradation of skin color depending on their distance from the equator; on both sides of the equator and closest to it live the darkest Negroes; in the African regions farther away from the equator the colors lighten all the way to the relatively pale complexion of the Hottentots. Where the coloration of the present tribes does not correspond with the climate of their habitat, this difference, according to Buffon, is to be explained either by migrations or by the length of time required to make the effect of the climate visible.[17] Buffon maintains that it takes about eight to twelve generations to bring about the darkening or bleaching of the skin.[18] The uniformity of the Indian tribes that have spread over the entire American continent without differentiation into races must therefore be explained through their relatively recent immigration by way of the Aleutians; the settlement of America could have taken place too recently to allow racial differentiation based on climate.

Buffon arranges all color classes on a color scale extending from white to black, and white is considered the basic complexion from which all other colorations have developed under the influence of the climate: "La chaleur du climat est la principale cause de la couleur noire." [A hot climate is the principal cause of a black color.][19] And: "Le blanc paraît donc être la couleur primitive de la Nature, que le climat, la nourriture et les moeurs altèrent et changent, même jusqu'au jaune, au brun ou au noir." [White, then, appears to be the original color of Nature, that climate, diet, and customs alter and change to yellow or brown or black.][20]

§5. The Unified Nature of Man

This explanation of the causes of racial diversity leads Buffon back to the realization of the unity of the form type from which they have split off. According to Buffon, various causal factors have led to the development of deviations from the original human form, the norm. These deviations differ more or less widely from the norm. From

16. *Ibid.*, 204.
17. *Ibid.*, 263.
18. *Ibid.*, 325.
19. *Ibid.*, 328.
20. *Ibid.*, 293.

this point of view, all human varieties are on the same level; they are all causally derived from the unified type. Following this insight Buffon's terminology in his summarizing statements becomes simpler and in its content comes close to the clearly defined concepts we will find in Kant's race theory. Indeed, Buffon's earlier comments now culminate in the proof that mankind, *le genre humain*, is not made up of basically different species, *espèces d'hommes*, but instead people are of one kind, one species, *espèce*, which has reproduced and spread over the whole earth.[21] In the course of spreading throughout the world the human species underwent many modifications due to the above-mentioned influences and to crossbreeding. At first the modifications were not very marked but only individual variations; as they became more common, pronounced, and established, they developed from differences in degree to differences in kind [*Artunterschiede*]. And according to Buffon, under unchanging external conditions they are now passed on from generation to generation, just as malformations or diseases are transmitted from parents to children. Since these differences developed over long periods of time under the influence of constant external causes, they can also disappear again if these causes would cease to exist, and mankind could then take on other forms than the current ones or it could even return to its norm.

Buffon uses the concepts of species and variety in this context in a fairly precise scientific sense; *species* and *varietas* are the lowest units for classification familiar from botany and zoology, and in Buffon's time they had already often been thought through methodically. Thus, we see here the first attempt to superimpose a purely scientific explanation of physical diversity on the description of the empirical bodily-spiritual human types, which as unified wholes are determined through the spirit. This scientific explanation does not yet entirely obscure the phenomenon of spirit, as it does in some modern race theories, because the idea of man as a unified essence based on his *ratio* is not yet given up; however, the possibility of turning the given types through scientific interpretation into antihistorical political ideas is already discernible.

Summarizing Buffon's theory, we can say that it is a speculative and notable mixture of the rational idea of man that was typical of

21. *Ibid.*

the eighteenth century and a biological concept of man as a creature determined by natural causality—a problem that was not fully thought through before Kant. According to the rational idea, Buffon is not so concerned with the exact description of the various different human types as with the presentation of mankind in its rich diversity. He stresses not the variety but the unity in which the differences appear, and for him the relationship between unity and diversity is that between the norm and the deviation from it. Therefore, the central idea of Buffon's description of people from all over the world is the systematic classification of the races according to their degree of deviation from the norm. The diverging subdivisions are defined through the causal factors leading to the deviation. Humanity is a single entity, created by God in His image, but it is subdivided in such a way that certain human groups—the European ones—achieve the norm or at least come very close to it, while others—the colored ones—remain more or less far from the norm. The racial classification is two-dimensional, based only on the distance from the norm; the selection of traits used for the classification is determined by the interest in the unusual, the strange, the exotic.

Here the rationalist-Christian concept of man as the crown of creation, the creature distinguished by his immortal soul and raised above all other beings on earth is blended with the foreign idea of including man in the animal kingdom. This latter idea, however, remains foreign, an admixture, and does not replace the concept of the unity of the human kind. The frequent use of the scientific concepts of species, variety, and race does not yet lead to a logically consistent, detailed classification of people according to physical traits as the ones determining the essence, and indeed, the distinctive essence of man.

5

The Classification of Races: Herder

Division of body & soul

The construction type of Buffon's race theory is relatively simple, and its ramifications and the possibilities it offers for new constructions can easily be seen. Its foundation is the Cartesian division of body and soul. And superimposed on this is the view of man as a unified whole of physical, characterological, and spiritual traits that appears on earth in many different forms. These two contradictory constructions are more or less joined in that at one time the inclusion of man in the animal kingdom is presented as a conventional classification that does not affect the true ontic status of man as a rational soul substance—that is, the contradiction is covered up in favor of the soul—at other times the explanation of the many variations of the whole through the climate also pulls the soul into the sphere of nature—that is, the emphasis is on the animal side. Buffon provides neither a clear analysis of the unavoidable speculative difficulty nor a clear division that would solve it perforce in favor of one or the other side.

With this situation as our starting point, there are two constructive possibilities. We can either let the soul substance dominate and declare the diversity of races irrelevant compared with many forms of the whole, the spiritual unity, or we can shift the emphasis to the causal-scientific explanation of the physical diversity and completely ignore the problem of the spirit and its connection to the body or completely separate the spirit from the body and treat its problems as independent of the physical diversity. One of these possibilities is realized in Herder's race theory, the other in Blumenbach's and Kant's. However, neither Herder nor Kant (nor Blumenbach) present these construction types in their pure—that is to say, one-sided—form; rather, they are presented only as predominant lines of thought in an extraordinarily organized speculative field. This is even more true for the less constructive and more intuitive

Herder than for Kant, who denied himself many a possibility in order to keep the lines of the system clear.

Turning first to Herder, we need a brief outline of the speculative lines forming the background to his race theory so we can understand Herder's position on race. And it seems to me that in spite of the large number of monographs—and among them many brilliant works—about Herder and his ideas on the philosophy of the history of man, his incredibly thorough and rich speculative system has not been fully appreciated for its greatness and, above all, its superiority to Kant's rather paltry image of man. Perhaps this is because Herder's intuitive-historical way of thinking and his writing style, in which fantastic analogies sometimes run riot, lack the pathos of the strict abstractness that deals with the issues as harshly as Kant—under whose harsh treatment they sometimes lose their form.

Neither the Cartesian dichotomy of body and *anima* or *ratio* nor the Kantian division into sensory nature and reason is satisfactory for Herder—he sees more. As a philosopher of the Enlightenment, Herder, like Linnaeus and Buffon, also sees man as a rational person, raised above the animal kingdom because of his reason. But for Herder reason is not a substance that can be isolated and, freed of all connections to the senses, added on to the body or soma as a differential element. Instead, he sees reason as an autonomous, psychic-lawful essence, as the spiritual unity of man in the same sense I. H. Fichte later expressed in more clearly defined concepts. Herder's understanding of man as a unified spiritual entity is the starting point for the drastic, polemic difference between him and Kant. In Kant's theory of reason, reason is the differential element, a substance in itself foreign to the body and the senses, that develops toward ever greater perfection and that continues this development when it has cast off the earthly shackles. Thus, a straight line runs through the development of reason in this world and the next, and death is merely a relatively irrelevant event. In Kant's view, the rational person must continue with this unending development when freed from the body just as much as in earthly life. And life on earth does not seem to obstruct this development any more than the life hereafter.

Herder is also convinced of the development and, like Kant, believes that reason cannot attain perfection in this life; here man is always in a state of becoming, a bud of humanity, so to speak. It is

again — dualism

this life — reason in a state of imperfect

next life — reason is perfect

Herder believes in a meaningful earthly existence Not Kant

only death that brings the decisive change: the rational creature tied to the world of animals and the body becomes a free being. We do not know any details about his status but we have to believe that in this being the bud comes into full flower. Herder does not continue the line of development from birth through death to infinity but juxtaposes the conditions in this life and the afterlife as the imperfect one and the perfect one. Before death man is completely shackled by earthly life, but after death he is free and can develop without restraint. Herder's image of this transition from one status to the other is that of the metamorphosis of a caterpillar into a butterfly. On either side of the transition there is a whole human life; while we know the makeup of life on this side, that of the life beyond death is a matter of faith.

Inherent in Herder's integral view is the belief in the meaning of earthly existence, which for Kant is characterized by a disconcerting meaninglessness. We will discuss below in more detail the difficulties inherent in Kant's construction, difficulties Kant was well aware of but could not overcome. Here we will point out only that earthly existence is necessarily devalued if the line of development extends unbroken beyond death. For succeeding generations the achievements of a rational person end with that person's death. Thus, in earthly life reason can only reach the goal of its development in the genus, not in the individual. People thus always live their lives only for the coming generations, and all generations work only for that far distant last one that will enjoy on earth what its predecessors have worked for. While Kant found the meaninglessness of earthly life "disconcerting," Herder believes that "All the works of God have this property, that, although they belong to a vast whole, each is in itself a whole, and bears the divine characters of its destiny within it." Earthly destiny, however, is "some form of human happiness and manner of life," simple pleasure in the company of parents and children, the quiet breath of daily life as one complete in itself. "Humaneness and happiness, in this place, to this degree, as this link, and no other, in the chain of development that extends throughout the whole race"—that is the meaning of life. "What and wherever thou art born, O man, there thou art what thou shouldst be: quit not the chain, set not thyself above it, but cling to it firmly! Only in connection with it, in what thou receivest and giveth, and in thy activity in both, only there wilt thou find life and peace for thyself." Earthly life is here seen as one, unified, integral, and mean-ingful, a view that developed and matured to full clarity in the nine-teenth century.[1]

In Herder's use of the Cartesian dualism of body and human soul the *two* integral concepts of the this-worldly and the other-worldly rational person replace the *one* specific differential concept of the soul. The specific concept of the body is replaced by that of the meaningfully structured earthly figure (with which we need not deal here) and that of the living form as a manifestation of a genetic force. Taking up an idea from Harvey and Wolff (about which below in greater detail), Herder posits a "vital organic force" that becomes active as soon as the egg cell is fertilized and builds up the species-specific body out of matter. This invisible force reveals itself in the matter that becomes a living being before our very eyes. "It becomes visible in the mass belonging to it and must carry *the prototype of its appearance within itself*, no matter how or where from. The new creature is nothing less than the realization of an idea of creative Na-ture, which always thinks actively."[2] The vital force creates the form and continues to maintain what it has created; this *innate* life force permanently dwells in all the parts of the body it has formed. "It is present everywhere in the creature in many different ways, for only through this force is the creature a living whole, maintaining itself, growing, and acting."[3]

Here too it is striking how close these formulations are to I. H. Fichte's anthropology. If we replace the concept of genetic force, which Herder took from the biology of his day, with the concept of the real soul substance, we are faced with Fichte's idea of the body-soul that indwells its body in all its parts. The concept of body that in Herder's work emerges palpably from the dispute between epige-neticists and preformationists was recovered for our time in Sche-ler's anthropology. Herder carefully and painstakingly distinguishes this life force from "our soul's faculty of reason"; the soul, he argues, surely did not build up the body, which it does not know, but only makes use of it as of an imperfect instrument for its thoughts.[4]

1. Johann Gottfried von Herder, *Ideen zur Philosophie der Geschichte der Menschheit*, in *Werke*, ed. Heinrich Kurz (Leipzig, n.d.), III, 267–69.
2. *Ibid.*, 212.
3. *Ibid.*, 213.
4. *Ibid.*

This last statement leads us beyond pure description of the speculative schema and into the problem of relationships between the parts. In place of the body-soul schema, we find four stages: first, the meaningfully organized earthly form; second, the body, animated and formed by a vital force (I have skipped not only details but also essentials—such as what Scheler called the "drive" of plants and for which Herder regrets being unable to find a suitable word in the language—since they do not relate directly to the speculative problem of race). The third stage is man endowed with reason, and the fourth, the human condition in the life after death. The relationships between these forms of being, whole and integral in themselves, now had to be discerned, in particular the relationship between the diversity of people as spiritually unified wholes and their diversity as biological units.

In the speculative situation we have developed here the question of the relationship between man as biological unit and as a spiritually unified whole can find only *one* answer. Herder's basic philosophical attitude sees only the unified wholes in their environment (thus the extensive discussion of the connection between climate and soul capacities) and does not permit the formation of differential concepts. For Herder, man is not a composite of animal and spirit, but a fully rounded whole; categories taken from the animal kingdom must not be applied to him. The sixth book of *Ideen* presents an overview of the diversity of the human form, an overview that essentially coincides in structure and content with that of Buffon. The next book begins with the thesis that "Much as the forms of the human race may differ all over the world, they all nevertheless belong to one and the same genus man." The sketched out "picture of the nations" has only a provisional character, "just as the groups in it do not presume to be anything more than what the *templa* of the augurs were in the skies, delimited spaces for our eyes and aids to our memory."[5] The picture as such "does not belong to both the systematic natural history and the physico-geographical history of mankind."[6] Just as Buffon tried to present the classification of man with the animals as merely conventionalistic and without significance for his true status, so Herder now calls the classification of the

5. *Ibid.*, 196.
6. *Ibid.*, 200.

diverse human forms merely an aid for the overview and deems it without any consequences. But while this digression into conventionalism remained merely an episode in Buffon's work and man and all varieties of man were integrated into the natural system, Herder is fully aware of the problem present here. Although, as we have said, his presentation of human diversity follows Buffon's in arrangement and descriptive details, Herder nevertheless carefully avoids ever calling the differentiated groups "races." He speaks of populations, peoples, nations, tribes, lineages—but the term pertaining to the natural system is not used. And Herder's methodological formulation of that classification not as part of systematic natural science but of the physico-geographical history of mankind is simply excellent. Though the diversity is real, it is not a biological fact but is essential only for the differentiation of the spiritually unified human whole according to climates and regions. The human collective is, for Herder, the "nation." "Each people is a nation; it has its national character and its own language; though the local clime may have left its mark on some and spread a soft veil over others, this does not destroy the original structure and character of the nation."[7] The central organizing principle for both the human groups and mankind as a whole lies in the spirit. The spirit, however, is not an autonomous element but with its formative action reaches down into matter. Indeed, in Herder's idea the meaningful unity reaches even beyond the human form and harmoniously also embraces its geographic and climatic environment. The shape of the earth and the climate harmonize with the populations living within them. In view of this reality, division into races becomes pointless. Some authors, Herder notes, have dared to call "races" four or five divisions of mankind that were "originally based on geographic distribution or color, but I see no reason for using this term. Race refers to a difference of descent, which here either does not exist at all, or which subsumes in each of these geographic regions, under each of these colors, very different races."[8] He goes on to say that these four or five races do not exist on this earth: "The colors blend into each other; and seen as a whole, everything ultimately becomes only shades in one and the same great picture that extends through all regions and

Herder doesn't use "race"

7. *Ibid.*, 199–200.
8. *Ibid.*

ages of the earth."[9] If not everything in Herder's ideas is completely clear, this is due to the structure of the speculative situation. The language has no words that allow us to distinguish clearly between spirit and body as differential concepts and spirit and body as designating the unified form. When we speak of the spiritual-personal unified whole of man, the body inevitably and insistently intrudes into the clarification of this expression, and this even though the body is not just a part forming the whole together with the spirit but it is already this unified whole, just as the spirit is too. In the explanation of the unified whole as being body and spirit at the same time (though we are simplifying here and disregarding the richly detailed problem of the structure of matter, vegetative drive, animal-genetic force, and spirit), the terms *body* and *spirit* are used in the differential meaning familiar to us. They are inevitably so used because the unified whole is not an ultimate ontic reality but is a fundamental experience that becomes independent as a construction, *one* of many possible constructions that take the contradictory fundamental experiences of the parts of the total being [*Gesamtwesen*] as their point of departure.[10]

9. *Ibid.*
10. See the Introduction, §2, and the chapter entitled "Body-Soul-Spirit" in *Race and State.*

6

The Classification of Races:
Blumenbach and Kant

In our discussion of the ideas of Ray and Herder we have already covered so many essentials of Kant's race theory that we need only add a few more summarizing and supplementary comments. We could draw a straight line from Ray's ideas of a natural biological subdivision to Kant's concept of the system of nature, and from Ray's concept of essence in its sense as the cause of the outer appearance to Kant's concept of the procreative power as the constant cause in the forming of animal groups through descent. We are also prepared for our current discussion of Kant's views because they are the antithesis to the kind of race description presented by Buffon and Herder: in view of the unified whole of man, both provide a description of the variety of human forms, listing physical, psychical, and social aspects side by side. On the other hand, we have the notion, already implicit in Buffon's analysis of the causes of racial differences, namely, that man is a purely physical being and that the classification of traits can be limited to those of the somatic sphere. This second, somatic type of study is based on the conception of man as a form consisting outwardly of different parts—the body and the soul—with the result that the physical form can be meaningfully studied by itself. This is the conception we have called the isolating type of construction.

This type of race theory was advocated by Blumenbach and Kant at the same time. Both base their theories on roughly the same facts and constructive premises and each knew the other's work, so that not only were their thoughts closely related due to their direct intellectual contact with each other but their conclusions were parallel because they both started from the same point of departure. For both the gift of reason distinguishes man from the animal; this definitively establishes the contrast between man's inner essence and the

man diff from animal b/c of gift of reason

subhuman world. And for both the question of the structure of *ratio* is completely separate from scientific investigations of man's physical form. However, the inclusion of man in the natural order as we find it in Buffon and Linnaeus still lingers on here—especially explicitly in Blumenbach, but the purport of the inclusion has changed in principle. For while Linnaeus still characterized the human genus by the principle *nosce te ipsum* and placed this *differentia specifica* on a par with the primates' incisors, Blumenbach, though including man in the class of the primates, did so based on distinguishing physical features.[1] Thus, man is included in the classification of nature only as far as his physical form is concerned, not with his inner essence. Nevertheless, Blumenbach also mentions the characteristic of man as *animal instrumentificum,* another rendering of Franklin's "tool-making animal,"[2] but this characterization is intended to negate man's animal nature and to contrast man with the animals. For our discussion of Kant we will assume that his unbiological critique of reason is well known. Both Blumenbach and Kant try hard to come up with a methodologically pure definition of natural groupings. But Blumenbach, with his extensive knowledge of details, is somewhat skeptical about deciding on a decisive criterion; Kant is more dogmatic. As mentioned above, Blumenbach refers to Ray as the scholar who established interfertility, that is, the ability of individuals to interbreed, as the defining indication that they have a common line of descent. However, Blumenbach believes that this criterion is not always applicable and fears that in the final analysis the analogy of the total habitus must suffice for the definition of a species. According to Blumenbach, all related forms must be considered as belonging to the same natural unit if the differences between them can be explained by the natural causes of deviation from the *habitus* of a breed (*clima, victus, vitae genus*).[3] As we have already seen, Kant is stricter in his application of this criterion, and his dogmatism in this question has influenced Girtanner's

1. Johann Friedrich Blumenbach, *De generis humani varietate nativa,* 3d ed. (Göttingen, 1795), 2–3.
2. *Ibid.,* 54–55.
3. *Ibid.,* 70. On the principle of genus: "Adeo ut fere desperem, posse aliunde quam ex analogia et verisimilitudine notionem speciei in zoologiae studio depromi." [Almost at the point of despair, I was able from other sources than from analogy and verisimilitude to produce the notion of species in zoology.] Compare also p. 72. On the question of the causes of deviation from type, compare pp. 88, 93, 96.

application of the "Kantian principle" to a number of botanical and zoological issues. Kant also developed the classical formulas of this procedure: the system of nature is contrasted to the scholastic system, the nominal genera are replaced with real genera, *description* of nature as the noncommittal description of presently existing forms must be supplemented with natural history as a "natural science of origins."[4] Furthermore, Kant offered the first systematic justification for the use of the word *race* in connection with the description of man. Ray used the term once in the sense of generation or descendants. In Buffon the term appears frequently, as a synonym for the equally vague words *espèce, variété,* and *nuance;* Herder deliberately avoids the term in his classification because of its implication of the animal-like. Kant justifies his use of the word *race* at length. "What is a *race?* The word does not exist in a systematic description of nature; presumably the thing itself therefore is nowhere in nature. Yet the *concept* this expression designates is surely well grounded in the reason of any observer of nature who, in view of any inherited characteristic of different interbreeding animals that is not inherent in the definition of their genus, thinks of a common cause, specifically of a cause originally part of this breed of the genus. That this word does not occur in descriptions of nature (the word *variety* appearing in its place) cannot prevent the observer from finding it necessary where natural history is concerned."[5] The concept of race therefore necessarily must occur in a system of nature or a natural history in the Kantian sense. Mere descriptions of nature can make do with the concepts of *genus, species,* and *varietas,* all of which refer merely to groupings of different size and content in their logical interrelationships. Natural history, which studies causes, must form its own concepts that designate the causal relationships (in contrast to the descriptive-logical ones) within a grouping. Kant chooses the word *phylum* to designate the highest natural unit (defined by the criterion of interfertility among the individuals) and *race* to mean groups within the phylum that are related by hereditary traits and *type* [*Schlag*] for groups marked by traits that are not necessarily inherited (in addition to modifications this includes also those groups of traits we now know to be heritable but whose herita-

---

4. Kant, *Über den Gebrauch teleologischer Prinzipien in der Philosophie* (Philosophische Bibliothek, 1788), 149.

5. *Ibid.,* 150. Kant believes that the word *race* derives from the word *radix.*

bility was not known before the discovery of the Mendelian laws because of the complicated transmission, frequently not discernible in the phenotype.[6] The development that begins with Ray's concept of essence and pushes through the idea of the system of nature in opposition to the scholastic system here finds its conclusion both in its method and in its terminology. The expression *race* is no longer a vaguely applied synonym for variety but encapsulates a well thought out concept of a natural subdivision.

For the most part, Kant's and Blumenbach's subdivisions into races coincide, but while Kant regards skin color as the decisive trait for the formation of a group, Blumenbach looks at the details of skin structure, establishing the concept of the complexion— the harmonizing of skin color, hair color, and eye color—and adds to the picture of each race with his studies of the cranium. With Blumenbach, skull shape takes on the great significance for race theory it still has in our time. Blumenbach subdivides humanity into five varieties according to skin color—white, yellow, copper-colored, brown, and black. Kant comes up with four varieties in his subdivision: white, yellow, black, and copper-colored. Both integrate their groupings into a natural system, according to which the varieties, that is, the "races" in Kant's sense, are derived through climatic influences from the basic human form, the "phylum" in the Kantian sense. Blumenbach's system is less precise and makes one of his five "races" the basic race, which results in the following schema:[7]

A. Caucasica.

B. Mongolica.	C. Aethiopica.
D. Americana.	E. Malaiica.

The Caucasian race is placed at the head as the basic form because white must be seen as the primitive color for, Blumenbach argues, deviation to darker colors is easier than a change in the other direction. The Mongolian and Ethiopian races follow in the system after the Caucasian one because, according to Blumenbach, they are the extreme developments of the basic form; the American variation must be placed between the Mongolian and the Caucasian, the

6. *Ibid.*, 151.
7. Blumenbach, *De generis*, 286–87.

Malaysian between the Ethiopian and the Caucasian. As the terminology already reveals, this biological core of the subdivision is surrounded by a layer of other, older ideas that continue the tradition of Buffon's divisions. The races are not named simply according to their traits but according to their principal abode. Thus, the basis of the subdivision is in part also determined by the physico-geographic factor isolated by Herder. Moreover, the above-mentioned argument that the extremes and the intermediate forms derived from the neutral white in precisely this way is not the only reason for this particular arrangement of the subdivisions. Buffon's idea of the norm also plays a part in this. Blumenbach calls the Caucasian race the most beautiful human type and in particular claims that this group has the most beautifully shaped head, from which the extremes of ugliness—the Mongolian and Ethiopian—are gradually derived.[8]

Kant's subdivision has fewer details than Blumenbach's but is significantly more rigorous in the fundamentals of the system. Since for Kant phylum and race have the strict sense of natural history, as explained above, none of the four races listed can be the basic form of the phylum. While Kant does not exclude the possibility that individual specimens of the basic form still exist, he considers this very unlikely. He thinks it more likely that all of humanity has already developed into a *progenies classifica* through local influences and has developed its inherent traits in a particular direction, and it is thus incapable of further development. Therefore, according to Kant, we must assume that at one time a basic form of the phylum existed, which most likely lived in the temperate zone. The current inhabitants of this zone are presumably still closest to this basic form; from this neutral form the major races developed through modifications caused by the effects of extreme climates. The following table results from this train of thought:

Basic genus: White, with brunette coloring.
First race: light blonde (northern Europe).
Second race: copper-red (America).
Third race: Black (Senegambian).
Fourth race: Olive yellow (Indian).

8. *Ibid.*, 303–304.

In this division the geographic element takes second place, and climate, as the causal factor leading to the development of races, is in first place. The first race—blonde and light-skinned—is caused by the northern moist cold; the second—copper-colored Americans—by dry cold (Buffon, too, thought the red color of the northern Mongolians was due to the dry cold); the black race is caused by moist heat; the olive-yellow race, by dry heat. In this system description becomes secondary, and the table is based on the dichotomies of fundamental qualities of the climate: moist-dry, cold-hot.

Though Blumenbach's and Kant's subdivisions are primitive compared to our knowledge of the subject matter, the Kantian one in particular has two decisive advantages over *all* modern systems: (1) its methodology is clear and neat; and (2) it takes into consideration *all* inevitable questions of race theory. In a methodologically flawless way, Kant limits his theory to the physical sphere of man. Buffon's muddled position, which Herder clarified in the direction of a study of the total, supervital, inner being, is purified by Kant in the direction of an inquiry into the subspiritual, animal realm. The idea of the norm, which is still lingering in Blumenbach's work, is absent from Kant's theory. Kant's pure theory answers the question of the unity of phylum man and declares all men members of one phylum because otherwise interbreeding between races would not be possible. The only explanation for the fact that the offspring of parents from different races show traits from each parent is that the parents were harmoniously adapted to each other by virtue of having developed from a shared origin through the unfolding of shared seeds. Kant's pure theory answers the question of the origin of races with the theory of the partial development under different climatic influences and explains the immutability of races through the irreversibility of a natural development.[9]

Thus we have traced the basic outline of the development of the problem of species in the eighteenth century to its conclusion in the fully elaborated concept of the natural unity of individuals. In the second part of our study we will look at how the modern race

9. For a modern arrangement of races of a high methodological quality, see Eugen Fischer, *Die gegenseitige Stellung der Menschenrassen auf Grund der Mendelschen Merkmale* (Internationaler Kongress für Bevölkerungsforschung) (Rome, 1931).

idea gradually grew out of the problem of body and mind of the eighteenth century. Before we take up this new thought, however, we will discuss another topic in this context, one that Kant alluded to in his definition of the concept of race—namely, the topic of the history of the word *race.*

7

On the History of the Word *Race*

Borrowed from the French language, the word *race* slowly entered the German language in the course of the eighteenth century, and by the last quarter of the century it had clearly gained ground.[1] Hypotheses on the origin and meaning of the word abound, but today none is undisputed; nevertheless, two or three seem more probable than the others. Various philologists name different root words: the Latin *radius* (Baist),[2] *radix* (Ulrich),[3] *raptia, raptiare* (Körting),[4] *generatio* (Salvioni, Meyer-Lübke);[5] a Slavic word, *raz*, which means "type," "stamp" (Gröber, Canello);[6] the Lombard *raiza*, "line," "stroke," Old High German *reiza* (Diez);[7] the Arabic *ras*, "beginning," "origin," "head" (Baist, Dozy, and Engelmann).[8] According to current philological thinking, most of these hypothetical root words must be eliminated for reasons related to history of language and the laws of phonetics, leaving as possible derivations only those from *generatio*, from *raiza*, and from the Arabic *ras*.[9]

1. See the article "Rasse" in Grimm's *Wörterbuch*.
2. Baist, *Romanische Forschungen*, I, 108 (according to Gamillscheg, *Etymologisches Wörterbuch der französischen Sprache* [1928], article "race"). See also Körting, *Etymologisches Wörterbuch der französischen Sprache* (1908), "race."
3. Ulrich (*Zeitschrift für romanische Philologie*, VI, 557) believes that a compromise of the nominative *radix* and the accusative *radicem* serves to explain the Italian *razza*, the neo-Provençal *raza*, and the like (according to Körting, *Lateinisch-romanisches Wörterbuch*, 3d ed. [1907], §7716, "radix").
4. Körting, *Lateinisch-romanisches Wörterbuch*, §7773, "raptio, -are."
5. W. Meyer-Lübke, *Romanisches etymologisches Wörterbuch*, 3732, "generatio." On Salvioni's view, see Gamillscheg, *Etymologisches Wörterbuch*, "race," and Körting, *Lateinisch-romanisches Wörterbuch*, §4216, "generatio."
6. See Gamillscheg, *Etymologisches Wörterbuch*, reference to Gröber. Körting, *Lateinisch-romanisches Wörterbuch*, §7716, refers to Canello.
7. Diez, *Etymologisches Wörterbuch der romanischen Sprachen*, 5th ed. (1887), 265. See also Körting, *Lateinisch-romanisches Wörterbuch*, §7716; Grimm's *Wörterbuch*, "Rasse." Gamillscheg also agrees with Diez.
8. Baist, *Die arabischen Laute im Spanischen* (*Romanische Forschungen*, IV) (1891), 415; Dozy and Engelmann, *Glossaire des mots Espagnols et Portugais dérivés de l'Arabe*, 2d ed. (1869), 329.
9. Gamillscheg agrees with the hypothesis of *raiza*; Meyer-Lübke traces *race* back

Meyer-Lübke advocated *generatio* as the root of the word *race*. The Italian *razza* has cognate forms in older dialects, the Venetian *narazza* and Old Bellunesian *naraccia;* from the same root are also derived the Friaulian *ğarnatsie* and the Old French *generace*. Meyer-Lübke finds the derivation from *raiza* "conceptually difficult"; derivation from the Arabic *ras* fails because the Italian *razza* can be shown to occur earlier than the equivalent Spanish *raza*—as early as the work of Franco Sacchetti, a Florentine writer of the fourteenth century, and in the "Intelligenza," an allegorical-didactic poem written around 1400 and whose author may have been Dino Compagni.[10] Körting objects to Salvioni's and Meyer-Lübke's derivation from *generatio:* "the disappearance of *two* initial syllables hardly seems credible."[11] And, in contrast to Meyer-Lübke, Diez finds not the least "conceptual difficulty" in deriving the word from the Lombard *raiza,* meaning "line" or "stroke." The word, he notes, is a literal rendering of the Latin *linea sanguinis,* designating the bloodline of descent.[12]

Körting's objection to deriving the word from either *generatio* or *raiza* is that the words *razza, race,* and the like all belong to postmedieval language and that therefore their direct roots cannot be in either popular Latin or Old Germanic.[13]

Dozy and Engelmann in their above-mentioned *Glossaire des mots espagnols et portugais dérivés de l'arabe* present the thesis that the word originated in the Arabic language but do not provide any support for it. As first occurrence of the word *rasa* they list the *Cancionero de Baena,* the oldest and only truly Castilian courtly songbook, which contains songs of the poetic society at the courts of King John I, Henry III, and John II of Castile—that is, from about

---

to *generatio.* Kluge in his *Etymologisches Wörterbuch der deutschen Sprache* in the sixth edition of 1899 takes the Arabic *ras* as the root word, but in the tenth edition of 1924 he opts for *generatio.* Plate in his *Etymologisches Wörterbuch der französischen Sprache* (1931) cites both *ras* and *raiza* with a question mark. Pianigiani in *Vocabolario etimologico della lingua italiana* (1907) chooses *raiza,* as does Holthausen, *Etymologisches Wörterbuch der englischen Sprache,* 2d ed. (1927). Skeat in *An Etymological Dictionary of the English Language* (1910) and Hatzfeld-Darmsteter-Thomas in *Dictionaire général de la langue française* (1920) note that the origin of the word is uncertain. Körting in his *Etymologisches Wörterbuch der französischen Sprache* (1908) calls it obscure.

10. Meyer-Lübke, *Romanisches etymologisches Wörterbuch,* 3732, "generatio."
11. Körting, *Lateinisch-romanisches Wörterbuch,* §4216a, "generatio."
12. Diez, *Etymologisches Wörterbuch der romanischen Sprachen,* "Razza."
13. Körting, *Lateinisch-romanisches Wörterbuch,* §7716, "radix."

1380 to roughly 1450.[14] Baist writes at greater length about the word's development in Arabic. According to him, the early forms *res* (Andalusian) and *ras* (Castilian) presumably originated in the cattle trade in the Spanish-Arabic border districts and mean "a piece of cattle" or, in the plural, "cattle." "That *raza*—since the sixteenth century, with remarkable preservation of the toneless syllable, Italian *razza*, French *race*, German *Rasse*—is nothing else should already have been realized from the use of the Portuguese *res* with the same meaning: it is the abstract content of the Arabic word 'beginning,' 'origin' = 'head.' "[15]

From this overview we can hardly draw any other conclusion than that the origin of the word *race* is uncertain. The improbability of two initial syllables having been dropped speaks against a derivation from *generatio*; the lack of continuity between the use of the early medieval word and the late medieval or post-medieval appearance of the word *race* argues against derivation from *raiza*. The hypothesis of an Arabic origin seems more likely because of a plausible connection based on the history of the language. However, Meyer-Lübke's argument that the word appears in Italian at the same time if not earlier argues against it. There is no indisputable record of an unbroken route of migration from Spanish to Italian, nor is there one for a migration in the opposite direction. This question can perhaps not be decided until the history of the Romance word, and in particular the Spanish one, is known in more detail. There is no dictionary of Italian or Spanish that is equal in quality to Grimm's dictionary of the German language. We have to be content with knowing that the word is of southern European origin, appearing at more or less the same time in the late fourteenth century in Italian and Spanish, from where it migrated to the other European languages.[16]

The word makes its way into French in the early sixteenth cen-

14. Dozy and Engelmann, *Glossaire*, 329, "rasa."
15. Baist, *Die arabischen Laute*, 329, "Rasa."
16. Compare the chapter on the origin of the word *race* in Schemann, *Die Rasse in den Geisteswissenschaften: Studien zur Geschichte des Rassengedankens* (Munich, 1928), 29ff. Schemann's work is essentially based on the same materials, but he distorts the facts tendentiously in favor of the German derivation. The distortion is found in the text on p. 29, but it is taken back in the note on p. 32—thus, all needs are satisfied: the wish for a German root of the word *race* in the text, the stirrings of an intellectual conscience in the note. Because of Schemann's sleight of hand in his treatment of the problems, his work should be used with caution and his sources should be checked carefully.

tury, from French into English at the end of the sixteenth century, from French into German in the eighteenth century. From its first appearance, the meanings of the word revolve around the fact of descent or origin. In one of the earliest documented French passages it has the meaning of offspring;[17] Ronsard uses it to mean generation;[18] another author gives it the meaning of fruits in the botanical sense.[19] The word means "descent" in Racine's line, "Une profonde nuit enveloppe sa race?" (*Athalie,* Act 3, Scene 4). We find the same meaning in the idiomatic expressions *noblesse de race* and *roture de race. Race* is further used to designate the French royal house (*première race,* and so forth).[20]

Skeat cites Spenser's *Faerie Queene* as the first English reference. The first three books of this work were published in 1590, and the relevant passage occurs in Book I, Canto 10, stanza 60:

> And thou, fair imp, sprung out from English race,
> However now accounted Elfin's son,
> Well worthy dost thy service for her grace,
> To aid a virgin desolate, fordone.

I found another use of the word in Spenser's dedication of "The Ruins of Time" to the Countess of Pembroke: "I have conceived this small poem . . . specially intended to the renowning of that noble race, from which both you and he sprung" (1591). In both passages the word has the meaning of tribe, house, or family. In the above-mentioned passage from Ray's *Discourses* the word means generation or offspring.

17. Angélique Desportes: "Race des Dieux de France, honneur de l'univers / Mon prince, mon seigneur, le support de mes vers" [Race of the Gods of France, honor of the universe / My prince, my Lord, the support of my verse]. Cited in Littré, *Dictionnaire de la langue française* (1872), article entitled "race."

18. "Car tout l'avoir mondain, quelque chose qu'on fasse, / Jamais ferme n'arreste à la troisième race." [For all worldly possession, whatever one does, / I always stop short at the third race.] Cited in Littré, *Dictionnaire.*

19. O. de Serres: "Contemplés curieusement les especes des raisins qu'y verrés, afin d'en tirer, en la saison, des races, s'il y en a, qui vous agreent." [You contemplate with curiosity the species of raisins you see for the purpose of drawing from the races if there is one that agrees with you.] Cited in Littré, *Dictionnaire.*

20. See, for example, B. Bossuet, *Polit.,* VII, VI, 14: "Les enfants de Clovis n'ayant pas marché dans les voies que saint Rémy leur avait prescrites, Dieu suscita une autre race pour régner en France." [The children of Clovis have not walked on the paths prescribed by Saint Remy, [so] God raises up another race to govern France.] Cited in Littré, *Dictionnaire.* [Voegelin's personal copy of the present work on p. 75 marginally notes: "Bacon, Essay XXIX, '. . . a race of military men . . .'" This essay was first published in 1612.—Ed.]

In German non-scientific common language the word seems to have infiltrated from the French with a definite sense of a value judgment. We have already seen that Herder vehemently refused to call the classification of man a division into races because human societies are not groupings like those of the animals. In addition to this factual reason, however, his rejection of the term also represents a value judgment, for he considers the animal sphere, where the word *race* may be appropriate, to be of lesser value than the human sphere. To speak of human races seems to Herder a degradation of man. In book 4, chapter 5, of *Ideen* we find the passage, "Gingen wir wie Bär und Affe auf allen Vieren, so lasset uns nicht zweifeln, dass auch die Menschenrassen (wenn mir das unedle Wort erlaubt ist) ihr eingeschränkteres Vaterland haben und nie verlassen würden" [Did we walk on all fours, like bears and apes, we cannot doubt that the human races (if I may use so ignoble a term) would have their limited fatherland and would never leave it] (p. 120). The word is evidently felt to pertain to a coarse, vital, physical realm and is therefore considered inappropriate and not quite decent when applied to human beings. There are many records documenting this coarse, slangy character of the word. In *Götter, Helden, und Wieland* (1773) Goethe has Charon say to Mercury, who comes to Kozytus with two shades, "Saubre Nation! Woher? Das ist einmal wieder von der rechten Rasse. Die könnten immer leben." [Splendid nation! Wherefrom? That is again from the right race. They could live forever.] It is probably impossible to render the nuance of meaning in this passage exactly, but the paraphrase "That is a fine one again" may come close. In *Wallensteins Lager*, Scene 6 (1797–1798) the meaning of the term is not so much deprecating as coarse:

> *Wachtmeister:* Ja, ihr gehört auch so zur ganzen Masse.
> *Erster Jäger:* Ihr seid wohl von einer besondern Rasse?
>
> [*Master of the Watch:* Well, you're just part of the great mass.
> *First Hunter:* And you, you belong to a special race?]

And in Schiller's translation of *Macbeth* (1800), Act 3, Scene 1, we find the word *race* used similarly but with a slightly more positive connotation when Macbeth replies to the First Murderer's cry, "We are men, my liege" with:

Ja, ja, ihr lauft so auf der Liste mit!
Wie Dachs und Windspiel alle Hunde heissen;
Die eigne Race aber unterscheidet
Den schlauen Späher, den getreuen Wächter,
Den flücht'gen Jäger. So auch mit den Menschen.

[Aye, in the Catalogue ye goe for men,
As Hounds, and Greyhoundes, Mungrels, Spaniels, Curres,
Showghes, Water-Rugs, and Demy-Wolves are clipt
All by the Name of Dogges: the valued file
Distinguishes the swift, the slow, the subtle,
The House-keeper, the Hunter, every one
According to the gift, which bounteous Nature
Hath in him clos'd: whereby he does receive
Particular addition, from the Bill,
That writes them all alike; and so of men.]

Here the meaning of *eigne Race* seems almost to be that of "particular descent"; the way the image is used shows the gradual transference of the increasingly positive connotation from the animal sphere to the human one.

The linguistic-historical situation is particularly evident in the first and subsequent editions of Blumenbach's work, *De generis humani varietate nativa.* The book is written in Latin, and how far the term *race* has penetrated into the German language is reflected in Blumenbach's Latin in the way the word *gens* is used and has changed its meaning. In the first edition of 1776 the human races are still designated by the traditional term *varietas,* and when the word *gens* appears, it has the ethnographic meaning of a people—as, for example, in the sentence, "Sintne fuerintne omnis aevi omnisque gentis homines unius ejusdemque diversaeve plane specie?" [Do men of every age and every race belong or have they not belonged to one and the same species, or to wholly different species?] The phrase *omnis aevi omnisque gentis homines* is the Latin form of the expression "men of every age and race." In the third edition of 1795 the words *varietas* and *gens* and their earlier meanings still occur but much less often than the word *gens* and the adjective *gentilitius* derived from it. Both virtually oust the former terms and are obviously stressed so much because of their meaning of "descent." The name for the five principal races remains *varietas: generis humani varietates quinae principes, species vero unica* [five principal human races, but a single species] (p. 284), and the word *gens* doubtless still retains the meaning of "people" or "nation," for example, when yellow skin color is said to be "Mongolicis gentibus familiaris" [typical for Mongolian people] (pp. 120–21). The meaning is more ambiguous in such phrases as *varietates coloris gentilitiae* [varieties of racial color] (p. 119) or *facies gentilitia* [racial faces] (pp. 174 ff.). And there can be no doubt at all that the word *gens* is replacing *varietas* when the adjective *gentilitius* is joined with the noun *character*, "trait," and a face is described as excellent *gentilitio quodam charactere* [in virtue of a certain racial character] (p. 196). In keeping with this concept of trait there is a *judaeorum facies gentilitia* [the racial face of Jews] (p. 196), a *craniorum forma gentilitia* [the racial form of the skull] (p. 197), a *norma verticalis ad characteres gentilitios craniorum definiendos* [a vertical norm for defining racial characteristics of skulls] (p. 203), a *habitus gentilitius* [racial condition of the body] (p. 319), and a *figuratio gentilitia* [racial shape] (p. 317). Apparently, the adjective "racial" was formed earlier in Latin scholarly language than in German.

As in Kant's and Herder's works, the word *race* still has an animal-biological connotation for Blumenbach. He even explicitly protests that his examination of facial bones for distinguishing racial traits, the study of *facies*, should not be misunderstood as a physiognomic attempt, a study of the *vultus*.[21] The word *race* attained the meaning familiar to us in the contemporary humanities only after the basic metaphysical conception of human nature had changed radically. This change is the topic to be discussed in the following sections.

---

21. Blumenbach, *De generis*, 182: "Ante omnia monere opportet hic loci non esse sermonem de vultu, physignomico sensu sumpto; temperamenti indice, qui quidem et ipse nonnumquam gentilitius et quibusdam nationibus proprius atque ex communi fonte derivendus esse potest." [Before everything there is required a warning that in this place there is no discussion of facial expression, taken in the physiognomical sense; to indicate temperament, which itself is never racial and proper to certain nations and is able to be derived from a common source.]

PART II

THE INTERNALIZATION
OF BODY AND PERSON

Part I of our investigations has shown the types of constructions that determined the thinking in the speculations about the problem of species in the eighteenth century. Ruling as the basic construction is what we have called the isolating type—the type in which the physical and soul components of the whole human form are so completely isolated from each other that they no longer have any essential elements in common. By treating each part of the human being as autonomous, this type of construction allows man to be considered as one of the animals and to be included in the classification of nature without denying the uniquely human spiritual being by inclusion in the subhuman world. In Herder's *Ideen* another type comes to the fore more strongly: the type of the unified form, with its subtle distinctions of geographical conditions, plant, animal, and this-worldly and otherworldly human being. As a method, however, the second type of construction was not as important as the first one. Though we could point out parallels between Herder's ideas and the idea of the unified form subsequently developed by the young Fichte, and though in its historical scope Herder's speculation undoubtedly offers the first great glimpse of the phenomenon of totality, its expression is still obscured by the dominant speculative *habitus* (orientation) of the eighteenth century, that is, the isolating construction. This subordination under the isolating type of construction was less obvious when we compared Herder's thinking with that of his time; in this comparison—with Kant, for example—the idea of the totality shines forth . . . we must look at Herder's edifice of ideas by itself, and then we can see the characteristic break in the hierarchy of being he has formulated, the break Kant made the object of his attack in his critique of Herder's *Ideen*. In this hierarchy each level of life forms—plants, animals, man—is ranked above the preceding one as ever higher manifestations of creative nature. Each complete form fulfills its life on its particular level of existence. Thus, *nature* ascends through the sequence of its manifestations, but *not* the *individual*. From the point of view of the individuals living on it, each level of existence is complete in itself. However, Herder changes this principle where man is concerned: man's rank of natural-divine manifestation is not followed by a higher one of beings of another kind, but by a new status of being, in which individuals participate when they have departed from their earthly life. Man is an "in-between creature," as Herder put it; he

89

stands in the middle between the animals and a form of being higher than man. This break in the construction reveals the dominance of the isolating construction; man's earthly corporeality, even if it is considered different from that of the animals because it is imbued by spirit, is nevertheless a residue that must fall away from the truly human being so that man can unfold his true nature—pure spirit— without restraint.

In this metaphysical thinking, race speculations of the sort we are familiar with today are still impossible; those require a basic reciprocal spiritualization of the body and embodiment of the spirit into the union of earthly-human existence as their foundation. In spite of the Enlightenment and the secularization of religious ideas, the speculations in the eighteenth century were without exception still oriented away from earthly life [*erdflüchtig*] and toward a higher, transcendent life of man in the Christian sense. The inner core of man's being was seen as lying not in his existence in this world but in his life in the next one. In this second part, entitled "Internalization" of the concepts of body and spirit in the sense of a shifting of the core of man's being from the transcendent realm into the inner being of this-worldly life, we will look at how the thought images of organism and finite person gradually grew out of eighteenth-century speculation and culminated in the new, this-worldly idea of man as a unity.

A. THE INTERNALIZATION OF THE BODY

8

Preformation and Epigenesis

Let us recall Ray's ideas; the outstanding and for us so valuable feature of his position as a thinker was his neutrality on the controversies of his time, in particular on the problem of preformation and epigenesis. He did not take a stand on the question of whether all individuals are already present in the first individual, with the act of procreation being merely the impetus to their growth, or whether God intervenes each time at the moment of conception to ensoul matter that in itself is lifeless. Ray acknowledged that arguments could be made for either explanation, and he left the question unresolved. It is precisely because he did not get lost in the details of defending any one position that we can see in his work the ideas underlying both explanations. Both solutions are rationalistic in the sense that the development of the organic form is not seen as a primary phenomenon; instead, this form is supposedly fashioned like a tool by a rational mind. Either God created all organisms at the same time and artfully fit one within the other or he creates each one anew at the time of conception. We recall that Ray in any case and definitively excluded the possibility that the parent animals could have anything to do with the creation of the new organism because, as he argued, they were not "aware" of it and because creating so artful an apparatus far exceeded their capabilities. Here the organism is conceived of as an artifact, created through rationally planning reason. The living form is not alive out of the wellsprings of its own vitality but is a machine put together from the outside, a mechanism; the principle of its development does not lie within the living form itself but rather takes hold of lifeless matter and shapes it mechanically into the apparatus we call animal or plant or man.

Albrecht von Haller was the classic proponent of this rationalistic theory on the preformationist side. In a kind of overview of the history of dogma, he explained that according to Jan Swammerdam

and other proponents of this theory the egg cell encloses a germ—
that is, a small fully formed human machine—and the bodies of all
human beings were fully formed and fitted into each other in Eve's
ovaries.[1] Here we have the pure form of the encapsulation theory, according to which all future generations, in an infinite series, lie fully
formed encapsulated within the ovum of the progenitrix, waiting
only for the moment when they will be able to develop, and that is
why this theory is also called evolution theory. In addition to the encapsulation theory in its pure form there were other kinds of explanations—for example, that at the creation of the world all bodies,
though as infinitely small germs, were created simultaneously and
then developed whenever external circumstances were favorable.
That is, they were not contained in the ovaries of the progenitrix but
were distributed all over the world, becoming visible as they developed.[2] Or: that all solid parts of the body are already fully formed but
still invisible in the earliest stage of the embryo and gradually become visible when fluid enters into them and expands the parts and
gives them volume.[3] Or: that the seed issues from all parts of the human being, a virtual copy of it in miniature, which thus explains the
similarity of the inner structure as well as the likeness of the external countenance. (Today, Darwin is credited with this theory, now
called "pangenesis"; he probably developed it in ignorance of his

1. Hermann Boerhave, *Hermanni Boerhave Praelectiones Academicae*, in *Proprias Institutiones rei medicae edidit, et notas addidit Albertus Haller*, V, Pt. 2,
"Menstrua Conceptus" (Göttingen, 1744), 498: "Sed evolutionum theoria obtinet a
Swammerdamio." [But the theory of evolution obtains from Swammerdam.] He and
many others "in ovo quidem germem, sive machinulam humanam perfectam dicent
includi. . . . Neque pauci eorum in ovario Evae hominum corpora formata et com-
plicata creata esse aiunt" [will say that indeed a germ, or a perfect little human machine, is included in the egg. . . . Nor do just a few of them say that the formed and
complicated bodies of men were created in the ovaries of Eve].

2. *Ibid.*, 498: "Sensim vero demum evolvi, quando in proprium et faventem locum incidunt, in quo ali possint, neque in ovario primae matris, sed ubique in orbe
terrarum dispersas latere." [In truth gradually they evolve at length, when they fall on
the proper and favorable place, in which others may be able to lie, and not in the ovary
of the first mother, but dispersed everywhere in the world.]

3. *Ibid.*, 497: "An omnia viscera, et musculi, et solidae reliquae partes quidem in
primis initiis invisibilis embryonis humani adfuerint, atque successive demum ad-
pareant, ubi ab influente humore paulatim dilatata, molem nacta fuerint visibilem."
[Whether the internal organs, and muscles, and indeed the rest of the solid parts were
present in the first invisible beginnings of the human embryo, and at length appeared
successively, where, extended by the inflowing humor, they became a visible mass
once born.]

predecessors.)[4] What all these hypotheses have in common, according to Haller, is that the structure of the body is already preformed in the embryo and is later only enlarged through warmth and the absorption of moisture.[5]

The so-called epigenetic theory of the origin of living forms does not differ from these variations of the preformist or evolutionist theory as far as the basic idea of inorganic matter is concerned. Descartes' theory can serve as an example. According to it, the fetus is formed in a process of fermentation. When the male and female germ fluids [*Keimsäfte*] have mingled, warmth initiates a process that is similar to the one occurring in new wine or in hay that has been brought into the barn when it is still too damp. In this process the particles of matter change unevenly. Some rush toward each other, unite, expand, and the pressure they exert on other particles creates the heart, which begins to beat. The fetus thus formed continues to develop according to the laws of mechanics. Thus the two theories agree in their mechanistic interpretation of organic development; they differ only in where they locate the beginning point of this mechanical development. According to the preformist theory, the image of an artifact appears at this point while in Descartes' theory the image is that of chemically caused development. Common to both, however, is the crucial element that the explanation is not based on immanent qualities of organic substance but on forces that work from the outside on lifeless matter and bring it to life.[6]

4. *Ibid.*, 497: "An demum semen, ex omni parte maris aut feminae, aut utriusque defluens, iconem quasi harum partium modulo expressam induat, atque adeo similitudinem parentum internam in fabrica, tum externam in facie exprimat?" [Whether at length the seed, flowing from every part of the male or the female, or that of both, bears in itself as it were expressed in diminutive the image of these parts, and to that extent expresses the likeness of the parents internally in the structure and externally in the face.]

5. *Ibid.*, 499: "qui omnes in eo conveniunt, ut fabricam totius corporis in embryone primigenio delineatam statuant, quam demum calor, et resorbtus humor, expandat" [who all agree in this, that the state that the structure of the whole body is in the first-begotten embryo, which is at length heat, and reabsorbed humor, expands].

6. René Descartes, *Tractatus de formatione foetus: Opera omnia*, III (Amsterdam, 1686), §28: "Primum autem quod in ista spermatum mixtura fit, quodque efficit ut guttae omnes desinant esse similes, est quod calor in eo excitetur, qui eodem modo agendo quoque in recentibus vinis dum effervescunt, aut etiam in foeno quod non bene siccatum in horreum conditum fuit; calor, inquam, ille efficit, ut nonullae eius particulae versus aliquem locum spatii in quo comprehenduntur coeant, ibique se dilatando, ambientes alias comprimant; quo pacto cor incipit formari." [But the first thing that happens in this mixture of sperm, and which makes it so that the droplets

Though in the scientific debates of the time these two theories were treated as irreconcilable opposites, we can see how close they actually were to each other because in the course of the discussions one blends into the other. This is particularly evident in the vacillations in Haller's theory. In the above-cited notes to Boerhave's lectures he rejected for his part every form of the preformation theory he has presented (although, as he says, he was trained in it). He advocated the opinion that the solid parts of the animal form gradually out of the liquid parts *secundum certas leges* [according to certain laws]. *Leges autem istas minime definimus* [However, we do not define these laws at all]—still he is fairly certain that this has nothing to do with a process of fermentation, which would be much too violent for the delicate embryonic structure and which, furthermore, never results in anything organic. Thus the Cartesian explanation is avoided, but nothing takes its place—which remains vacant—and the epigenetic theory is limited to a description of the observable gradual growth of solid parts through the absorption of fluid.[7] From this position, which is less a theoretical stance than descriptive reservation, it is only a short step to the theory of evolution, a step Haller took based on his studies of chicken eggs. The description remains the same,[8] except that the fluid, not further qualified, from which the solid parts arise, has become *un fluide apparemment organisé*. This "apparently" organized fluid contains its own principle of organization, not yet as a force or drive but as a fully formed organ-

---

all cease to be similar, is that heat is excited in them, which, by acting in the same manner as also occurs in new wines while they effervesce, or also in not well dried hay found in a barn; heat, I say, brings it about that some of the particles are moved toward some place where they are contained, and, expanding themselves there, press upon others near them; once this has occurred the heart begins to be formed.]

7. Haller, "Menstrua Conceptus," in Boerhave, *Proprias Institutiones*, 500: "In plantis, sed perinde in animalibus manifestum est fibras (sed animalis solida nulla sunt praeter fibras) ex liquido generari. In arboribus succus humectus abit in cellulosam lanuginem, haec exsiccata in fila. Pulpa pomorum, farina triticorum etc. merus effusus et coactus succus est. [In plants, hence also in animals fibers are generated from liquid (but solid animals are nothing but fibers). In trees, the wet sap goes into down-like cells, and dried out this becomes a strand. The pulp of fruit, the grain of wheat, etc. is just sap poured out and compressed.]

8. Albrecht von Haller, *Sur la Formation du Coeur dans la Poulet*, Vol. II, *Précis des observations: Suivi de Réflexions sur le development* (Lausanne, 1758), 175: "Toutes les parties du corps animal naissant d'un fluide apparemment organisé, qui devient muqueux, et qui acquiert peu à peu des limites déterminées, et une consistance qui résiste à la pression." [All the parts of animals are born from an apparently organized fluid, which becomes mucous, and which little by little acquires determinate limits, and a consistency that resists pressure.]

ism whose parts only need to grow.[9] In his textbook on physiology, Haller unequivocally espouses creationism, arguing that the explanations of a random encounter of atoms or a fermentation process must be rejected just as much as the assumption of a constructing soul, which would be incapable of such a glorious work (see Ray's argument). "Therefore it seems to me certain that the excellent structure of animals . . . , which is calculated according to more perfect laws than are taught by all human skill in measuring and which at any rate seems obviously constructed for foreseen purposes in eyes, ears, and hands, can be put down to no lesser cause than the wisdom of the Creator. . . . This is all the more certain because what is visible in the fully grown animal existed already in the more delicate embryo."[10] Haller limits the contribution of the male semen in conception to a mechanical stimulus; it merely gives the embryo's tiny heart the impetus for its first contractions "so that by and by it unfolds the tiny vessels of the rest of the body, which are folded up, through the fluid driven into them and spreads the vital motion through all the channels of the animal's little body."[11] The epigenetic description thus follows the creationist preformation theory, and the two are combined into a comprehensive theory of the development of the individual.

Because the same ideas underlie these warring theories, we must see them as a unity and try to formulate here provisionally the ideal point of departure as well as the ideal goal toward which these theoretical edifices are moving through the metamorphoses of their meanings. To this end we juxtapose the transcendent attempts to explain the phenomenon of life with the immanent ones and arrive at the following definitions: Transcendent attempts are all those that try to explain unified life-forms through divine creation and the encapsulation of all subsequent generations within the originally created one as well as the mechanistic theories of the origin of life; in contrast, all those interpretations are immanent that see life as a

9. *Ibid.*, 186: "Il me parait presque démontrable, que l'embryon se trouve dans l'oeuf, et la mère contient dans son ovaire tout ce qui est essentiel au fetus." [It seems almost demonstrable to me that the embryo is found in the egg, and the mother contains in her ovary everything that is essential to the fetus.]

10. Albrecht von Haller, *Grundriss der Physiologie für Vorlesungen*, trans. and ed. from the fourth Latin edition by Sömmering and T. F. Meckel (Berlin, 1788), 654ff., §§884, 885.

11. *Ibid.*, 655–56, §886.

unique ontic realm and assume an instinctive agent along the lines of the genetic force posited by Herder, an agent that determines the character of the life-form. For race theory a consequence of the transition from the transcendent creationist or mechanistic interpretation to one based on a formative drive was that the problem of the nature and character of the human body [*Leibartung*] was shifted into that body itself. To explain it, one no longer draws upon transcendent authorities, such as God or the lifeless mechanical processes of nature; the body is neither an artifact nor a mechanism; instead, man appears as a psychophysical union that carries the defining characteristics for its living existence within itself. The transition from the transcendent interpretation of the primary phenomenon of life to the immanent one is an internalization of the body that parallels the internalization of the person, through which the end of the eighteenth century became an epoch in European history.

9

The Organism and the Animal in Itself: Wolff's *Theoria Generationis*

§1. *Vis essentialis* and *solidescibilitas*

In Haller's vacillation we already saw the older opposition between preformation and epigenesis begin to dissolve, a process that continues in Wolff's *Theoria generationis*, leading to an almost insoluble tangle of ideas because the transition to an immanent interpretation of life also takes place in this theory. The experimental and microscopic findings on which Wolff's theory is based are essentially the same as those Haller used. That is, the formation of the embryo becomes visible at a particular stage of development in the egg, but unlike Haller, Wolff is not inclined to assume that the presence of the embryo in the egg from the very beginning is *presque démonstrable*; instead, he rejects all speculations about the invisible preliminary stages. Though he concedes that one cannot categorically declare that what is not evident to the senses does not exist, he considers applying this argument to this issue more ingenious than apt. After all, the material particles that make up a germ cell can be clearly seen through a microscope and more powerful microscopes reveal nothing not shown by weaker ones. Therefore, Wolff sees no reason to speak of parts that remain invisible because they are too small to be seen.[1] This argument carefully separates

---

1. Caspar Friedrich Wolff, *Theoria Generationis:* Editio nova, aucta et emendata (Halle, 1774; first ed., 1755), §166, note: "Partes constitutivae, ex quibus omnis corporis animalis partes in primis initiis componuntur, sunt globuli, mediocri microscopio cedentes semper. . . . Nemo unquam eficacioris lentis ope partes detexit, quas non statim vilioris notae microscopi deprehenderit. . . . Absconditae igitur partes propter infinitam parvitatem, indeque sensim emergentes, fabulae sunt." [The constitutive parts, from which all the parts of the animal body are composed at the start, are globules, the moderate ones always accessible by the microscope. . . . By the work of a more efficacious lens, no one ever detected parts which the work of a more worth-

the entire visible development of the embryo's parts from the preceding phase, when nothing is visible and therefore, the argument goes, nothing exists. In a strictly empirical way this makes room for the theory of generation, which is to be understood as the *formatio secundum omnes suas partes, et modum compositionis illius ex hisce* [the formation according to all its parts, and the mode of composition of this or that part] of the organism's body.[2] Solid parts begin abruptly to grow out of fluids, just as Haller assumed, but the precondition for this process is not the already fully formed organism but rather a *principium generationis* [principle of generation], a *vis corporis qua illa formatio praestatur* [power of the body by which that formation is supplied], and the manner in which this force works leads to the *generationis leges* [laws of generation] sought by Haller.[3] According to Wolff, plant organisms are nourished and grow by taking in nutrient fluids. We can observe the absorption of liquids, their distribution throughout the plant, and finally their elimination, and all these effects are produced by a force that takes in the liquids from the surrounding soil through the roots, distributes it throughout the whole plant, in part depositing it and in part expelling it again.[4] This force must be assumed if one wants to claim that plants are nourished through the circulation of sap—*sufficiet ea praesenti scopo, et vocabitur vis vegetabilium essentialis* [this shall suffice for the present purpose, and shall be named the essential power of the plants].[5] This nourishing sap, Wolff suggests, evaporates sufficiently to become a somewhat thick, viscous, and finally solid substance; Wolff calls this characteristic *solidescibilitas* and considers it an essential property of the *substantia vegetans*.[6] The cell tissues grow when the thickening nutrient sap is deposited in them.

---

less kind of microscope did not immediately detect. . . . Therefore the parts hidden on account of infinite smallness, and so emerging insensibly, are the stuff of fables.]

2. Wolff, *Theoria*, "Praemomenda," §1.

3. *Ibid.*, §2.

4. Wolff, *Theoria*, §1: "obtinere . . . vim, qua humores ex circumjacente terra, vel aliis corporibus colliguntur, subire radicem coguntur, per omnem plantam distribuuntur, partim ad diversa loca deponuntur, partim foras expelluntur" [to obtain . . . the power, by which humors are collected from the surrounding land, or from other bodies, are compelled to go under the root, and are distributed throughout every plant, partly deposited at diverse places, partly expelled outside].

5. *Ibid.*, §4.

6. *Ibid.*, §§27, 234.

Wolff thus derives the totality of organic phenomena from the two principles of *vis essentialis* and the ability of vegetal substance to solidify.

§2. Conception as a Borderline Case of Nourishment

Once the basic phenomenon of body growth through nourishment has thus been explained, Wolff goes back to the origins of nourishment to understand the beginning of this process in all its features. He sets up a hierarchy of types of nourishment from the coarsest to the finest to explain the beginning of individual life through a particular process of nourishment. According to Wolff, (a) the adult person takes in a variety of solid nourishment, which is processed by the stomach; (b) the weaned child is given minced food, since the masticatory organs and digestive juices are not yet sufficiently developed; (c) the newborn child requires a form of food that is already prepared in another body—milk; (d) the fetus is nourished by juices supplied with the aid of the placenta; and finally (e) the sperm is supplied to the egg.[7] The growth of the individual begins with conception,[8] which essentially consists in the supply of a complete nutrient substance; the male sperm has a very high nutritional value.[9] Thus, conception is nothing more than *praeter suppediationem perfecti nutrimenti* [the supply of perfect nutrition], and sperm is nothing but *illud perfectum nutrimentum ipsum* [that perfect nutrition itself].[10] For growth to begin, the principles of the *vis essentialis* and the *solidescibilitas* are joined by the concrete event of vegetal substance being supplied.[11]

7. *Ibid.*, §230, note 4.
8. *Ibid.:* "Per conceptionem enim prima corporis stamina, spinae scilicet dorsalis, et capitis rudimentum deponuntur." [For by conception the first threads of the body, namely, the dorsal spine, and the rudiment of the head, are produced.]
9. *Ibid.*, §165: "Essentia conceptionis in mera perfecti nutrimenti suppeditatione seminis masculini vero in mera summi gradus facultate nutriendi consistit." [The essence of conception consists in the mere supply of perfect nutriment, and indeed the essence of the masculine sperm in the sheer nutritional faculty of the highest grade.]
10. *Ibid.*
11. *Ibid.*, §242: "Tum in plantis, tum in animalibus, ex sola vi essentiali, et solidescibilitate succi nutritii applicati, singulae illae vegetationis species derivatae sunt." [Both in plants and in animals, the single species of that vegetation are derived from the essential power alone, and from the capacity to solidify of the applied nutritive juice.]

§3. The Word *Organism* in the Sense of *Mechanism;* Preliminaries for the Change in Meaning

By going back through the hierarchical levels of nourishment the focal point of the problem of generation is set at the absolute beginning of conception, which is understood as a kind of nourishment. This primordial nourishment begins before the organic apparatus as we know it, with its digestive system, even exists. Thus the problem of generation is moved back to a time before the organism's existence. Wolff's discussions of this question are of special significance since that is where the transition from the concept of the organism as a mechanism to the newer notion of the organic element as something alive takes place. Interpreting generation as a preorganic process is not meant to present it as an event governed by mechanical laws; on the contrary, it is meant to present it as a life process as opposed to organic processes, which in the mid-eighteenth century were still considered mechanical ones. Wolff distinguishes between the organic body, which is the same as a machine, and the vegetal substance, whose elements—the *corpora vegetabilia*—are not *machinae* but *in*organic substances. The expression *inorganic* thus means here the exact opposite of what it means for us today—that is, "organic." The inorganic vegetal substance is the building material of the machine, that is, of the organism, to use Wolff's language; the organism is thus a deposit, a hardening of substance.[12] Thus the *vis motrix* or *vis essentialis,* that is, the generative principle, the force that governs plant metabolism, can be more clearly defined than was previously possible.[13] The *vis motrix* is thus neither a force inherent in the organism conceived of as a machine nor is it a principle of the nutrient liquids. Instead, it is a force that cannot be localized in any material component and whose relationship to these components is that of "application." The growth of the organism is not

12. *Ibid.,* §253.
13. *Ibid.,* §233: "Primum igitur generationis principium et quo agente omnia efficiuntur, est illa vis motrix, quam essentialem denominavi, plantis et animalibus vis necessaria. . . . Vim essentialem ego definivi, quod sit ea vis, qua humores per plantam distribuuntur, et excernuntur." [Therefore the first principle of generation by the agency of which everything is brought about is that motor power, which I have named "essential," the power necessary for plants and animals. . . . I have defined as the essential power, which is that power by which humors are distributed throughout the plant, and excreted.]

caused directly by the force inherent in it, *sed quatenus haec vis humoribus, in guttas collectis, contra solidum directis, applicata est* [but inasmuch as this power has been applied to the humors collected into drops and headed toward becoming solid].[14] The *vis essentialis* is completely removed from the material structure of the organism and turned into an immaterial principle.[15]

§4. Preexistence of the Animal in Itself— Mechanistic and Animalistic Functions

However, Wolff does not stop there; he makes an effort to allay the suspicion that the mechanical terminology of force and effect and application of force still means anything mechanical. He therefore distinguishes between the functions of the organism in the mechanical sense and the properly animal functions that make use of the or-

---

14. *Ibid.*

15. Rádl's presentation of Wolff's *Theoria generationis* in his history of biological theories is correct in its details but misleading in the main point. Wolff's great significance in the history of ideas lies in his development of a concept of the living form in opposition to the mechanistic interpretation of the body, which in his day was the prevailing view. And this effort had to be played out as a struggle against the concept of organism because the word *organism* at that time still had the meaning of mechanism. It is largely due to Wolff's work that the meaning of this word changed. On this fundamentally important point Rádl writes (p. 155): "In this chapter Wolff claims that the developing bodies have no structure at the outset, that their structure (machine) is merely the consequence of development: the essential force turns the originally unstructured substance into the ultimately extant form. This conception is expressed in the somewhat obscure statement that bodies in the process of development are not machines but merely consist of inorganic (= not organized) substance. And this developing substance must be distinguished from the machine in which it is enveloped. The machine must be seen as the product of the former." I wish to state on the contrary that this sentence is not the least bit obscure if we translate the vocabulary of that time properly into the modern terminology—thus, organized substance = dead matter, inorganic substance = living matter; the cited passage then states that living matter is deposited and forms the solid physical structure; but in the process of being deposited, it has also become unliving, it has become a machine. The "developing body" corresponds to Fichte's concept of the pneumatic living body [*Leib*] as opposed to the body [*Körper*] as dead matter. We will have more to say on this point in the text. I therefore suspect that Rádl did not understand the cited passage and the entire world of meanings it reflects. We may attribute this misunderstanding to the circumstance that Rádl did not take the trouble to read the work in the original, contenting himself with the frequently imprecise German translation (in Ostwald's *Klassiker der exakten Wissenschaften*, Numbers 84/85). It may well be that the translator also failed to understand the original, or he would not have neglected, in his introduction that discusses many aspects of lesser significance, to point out these shifts in meaning, which are indispensable to an understanding of the text but which in fact are not easily discernible in the translation.

ganism. The animal functions are to be understood as premechanical, since the "animal" "exists" embryonally even before the organism is fully formed. The "animal itself" must be distinguished from the machine in which it lives, and Wolff questions whether there can be any doubt that the mechanical actions are nothing more than an insignificant appendage of the animal itself.[16] In particular Wolff argues that the mechanical apparatus is not the essential aspect of the animal functions: it is not the mechanical effects of the stomach that are important but the function of digestion, which exists even before the stomach does. By the same token, blood is not created by the lungs, heart, and kidneys but exists already before this mechanism is formed; the embryo eliminates before it has a kidney to use, and the eye is an optical device clearly different from the sense of sight; and so forth.[17] However, according to Wolff, simply denying the mechanical nature of the animal functions does not accomplish much; a new interpretation of these processes is needed. Wolff was not able to deal with this question in detail or systematically, but his few indicative statements are sufficient to express his opinion clearly and unquestionably. Closest to his own view of the matter, he writes, comes the opinion that the bodily functions must be attributed to workings of an immaterial soul.[18] An immaterial soul is thus the agent of the living being, and to forestall the reader's reproach that the author contradicts in this explanation his theory presented in mechanistic terminology, Wolff adds that he presented the theory, which has a distinct mechanistic ring, in this form only to use the traditional concepts and ideas, but his intention has all

16. Wolff, *Theoria*, §255, Schol. 1: "quin omnes illae recensae actiones mechanicae solummodo ut levis quasi animalium appendix sint considerandae" [lest all those mechanical actions reviewed be considered only as sort of a frivolous appendix of the animals].

17. *Ibid.*, Schol. 3. See, for example, the statement that the destruction of the lens is "laesio collectionis radiorum, tamquam actionis mechanicae, non vero visus, tamquam actionis animalis" [a lesion of a collection of rays, as a mechanical action, but not sight, as an animal action]. Compare this with Scheler's analyses: only the optical apparatus receives rays of light; the "eye" as a sense organ "sees" colors.

18. *Ibid.*, Schol. 4: "sententia . . . , qua scilicet functiones in corpore nostrae peractae, arbitrio attribuuntur animae immaterialis, sive directricis et libere agentis, sive ex incommodo, ipsi illato, coactae" [the opinion . . . by which, that is to say, our functions performed in the body are attributed to the choice of the immaterial soul, whether of the directive and free agent, or whether coerced, from constraint, with the removal of that free agent itself].

along been to reveal the process of generation as something external that appears in connection with something internal, namely, the life of an *anima immaterialis*.[19]

§5. Summarizing Characterization

What is unique about Wolff's theory is its strong inner animation. The biological terminology is still that of transcendence, and Wolff attempts to express the immanent notion of the body through this medium. The concept of a materially and structurally preformed organism is replaced by that of the pre-existence of the "animal itself," the *animal ipse*—as it were, an *animal in itself*—that as immaterial soul determines the structure of the body. Thus an essential step has been taken toward the internalization of the body image, but it is not yet fully attained, since in Wolff's theory the body, following the metaphysical thinking of his day, is still split into two parts—the soul without matter, the *vis essentialis*, and the mechanism of the body, understood as purely substance. The Cartesian dualism of the subhuman machinelike body and the human soul is also applied to the sphere of animals and plants; though the animal is no longer a machine, it is also not yet purely organic but a mechanical body animated by the *vis motrix*. However, the exigencies of his subject matter prompt Wolff to go beyond what the pure isolating construction would permit; though the *vis essentialis* as an immaterial force without dimensions is juxtaposed to the whole body mechanism, in the exposition of the idea each mechanical function is correlated to a parallel "animal" function so that overall the mechanical and animal body nestled into each other make up the animal or plant. The concrete detailed discussion almost arrives at the idea of the spiritual body that is corporealized in matter; because an animal function is seen behind each mechanical function, the soul is seen to permeate the entire body. Mechanical and animal aspects appear as the

19. *Ibid.:* "Deinde, ne id vitio vertas, velim, nec videar mihi contradixisse, dum receptorum terminorum gratia ita in tota dissertatione locutus sum, quasi omnia mechanice peragerentur." [Consequently, I prefer that you not attend to it by default, and that I may not seem to have contradicted myself, even as in the whole dissertation I have spoken thus in behalf of the received terms, as if everything were performed mechanically.]

two sides of one ontic reality, and that is already almost the formula in which Scheler articulated his doctrine of the body in contradistinction to the Cartesian one. In spite of the clear juxtaposition of organo-mechanism and pre-existing animal in itself, the difficulties of expressing the idea in the traditional language of science remain so great that a consistent exposition of the idea is impossible, and instead mechanical notions of transcendence, the idea of the immaterial body, and that of the immaterial soul become oddly mingled.

10

Reinterpretation of Mechanism as Organism

The difficulties that had to be overcome to arrive at the idea and concept of a body that is in itself alive, and the significance of Wolff's *Theoria generationis* in this transition—in spite of a vitalist precursor of the stature of Georg Ernst Stahl—become clearer when we compare a concept of the organism from the beginning of the century with one from the end, with the middle of the century being characterized by Wolff's work. We will have to conclude from this comparison that in terms of practical concepts the treatment of the issue had hardly changed at all. I am thinking here particularly of the concepts of the organism held by Leibniz and by Lorenz Oken.

§1. Leibniz

For Leibniz, plant or animal life forms were composites of monads under the direction of a dominant entelechy, which functioned as the soul of the creature.[1] The monadic entelechy is an indivisible, simple, imperishable substance that originated in the act of creation of the world by God and can be destroyed only by a corresponding divine act of annihilation. Thus, given the world as fact, the monads are immortal. Leibniz reinterprets the rationalistic preformation of the body into the preexistence of the monad and accordingly sees generation and growth of the living being as nothing more than the growing of a body around this monad, the body's organizing principle. Life does not come into being and then perish; rather, what appears as life and death is a shift in the ordering of the monads around one dominant monad. The soul changes its body only gradually and

---

1. Gottfried Wilhelm Leibniz, *Monadologie*, §70: "On voit par là, que chaque corps vivant a une entéléchie dominante qui est l'âme dans l'animal." [By this one sees that every living body has a dominant entelechy, which is the soul in the animal.]

is never deprived of all its organs at once. The living animal under-goes a metamorphosis in the transformations of its body, but there is no metempsychosis, no migrating of the soul from one body into an-other, for there is no soul that is completely separate from a body.[2] What we call development and death of a body is merely a corporeal accretion and diminution around the center formed by the entele-chy.[3] *L'animal même,* the animal itself, is indestructible, though its machine often perishes. Here, essential points of Wolff's theory and terminology are already anticipated.[4]

The monad can never completely lose its body because it is both body and soul at the same time. According to Leibniz there is no sub-stance except monadic substance, and the "body" of the living being is not a kind of being in opposition to the dominating entelechy; rather it is the same entelechy only in different formation. Every-thing psychic [*seelisch*] is also physical, just as everything physical is also psychic. The monad presents us with the idea of "body" but in the terminology of an opposition between body and soul. "Organic bodies are never without souls, and souls are never separated from all organic bodies although there is no material part which might be said to belong always to the same soul. Therefore I assume neither that there are souls that are by nature entirely detached nor that there are created spirits that are entirely free of any body, a view I share with several Church Fathers. God alone stands above all mat-ter since he is its creator; if his creatures, however, were free and de-tached from matter, they would then be cut loose from the general interconnectedness and be like rebels against the general order."[5]

2. *Ibid.,* §72: "Ainsi l'âme ne change de corps que peu à peu et par degrés, de sorte qu'elle n'est jamais dépouillée tout d'un coup de tous ses organes; et il y a souvent métamorphose dans les animaux, mais jamais métempsychose ni transmigration des âmes: il n'y a pas non plus des âmes tout à fait séparées, ni de génies sans corps. Dieu seul en est détaché entièrement." [Thus the soul only changes the body little by little and by degrees, in a way that it is never deprived all at once of all its organs; and meta-morphosis often occurs in the animals, but never a metempsychosis or transmigra-tion of souls: there are no longer any utterly separated souls, nor spirits without a body. God alone is completely detached.]

3. *Ibid.,* §73: "C'est ce qui fait aussi qu'il n'y a jamais ni génération entière, ni mort parfaite, prise à la rigueur, consistant dans la séparation de l'âme. Et ce que nous appelons générations, sont des développements et des accroissements, comme ce que nous appelons morts sont des enveloppements et diminutions." [This also explains why there is never either complete generation or perfect death, taken rigorously, as consisting in the separation of the soul. And what we call generations are develop-ments and growths, just as what we call deaths are envelopments and diminutions.]

4. *Ibid.,* §77.

5. Gottfried Wilhelm Leibniz, *Betrachtungen über die Lebensprinzipien und*

The corporeality of the soul expresses its finite nature as created by God and linked in union with all of creation. The organic body of living beings is therefore an *espèce de machine divine* [species of divine machine], an *automate naturel* [a natural automaton], but completely different from any artifact in the sense of something produced by reason because in the artifact the distinction between the plan and the material in which it is executed is visible while the divine machines are ensouled through and through, from their smallest particles to infinity.[6]

This is a prime example illustrating how the will to see the body as a unique unity dashes against the habitual images and meanings of words that do not allow the body to be conceived of as anything other than an ensouled machine. The monad is neither body nor soul—that is, neither dead matter nor ensouling principle—but living body, an entity that does not fit into the categories of body and soul but that Leibniz nevertheless has to comprehend in terms of these categories. That is why he ends up with the curious construction in which the organism must be seen as a composite of material elements under the rule of a soul while at the same time both the material elements and the soul are also monads—that is, neither material nor soul but the desired third element, the unities of life. Thus, a machine in the mechanical sense emerges in these speculations that in its inner structure is not a machine in this sense after all; instead it is an organism. Leibniz expresses this idea with the terms *machine divine* and *machine artificielle.* The *machine artificielle*, the apparatus produced by man, is meaningfully organized only in its larger parts. The ultimate organized unit may be, for example, a brass wheel; its parts are no longer organized components of the machine but unformed, material elements. The machines of nature, living bodies, however, are machines down to their tiniest parts, and this is what differentiates God's handiwork from man's. By crossing this frontier into the infinitely small part of the apparatus, the concept of the machine undergoes a complete change in meaning. Normally it refers to matter shaped by man into a tool, an apparatus whose movements run their course according to a plan—the plan that was built into it. *Machine* and *mechanism* designate a

---

über die plastischen Naturen (1705), *Hauptschriften zur Grundlegung der Philosophie*, II (Philosophische Bibliothek), 73.
    6. Leibniz, *Monadologie*, §64.

system of movements whose laws of motion are transcendent compared to the actual moving apparatus. Through the transition of the concept *machine* to the realm of the infinite, from an external organization of matter to being completely ensouled down to the elements—that is, to the nullification of matter—the meaning of the word *machine* is transformed into that of *organism.* While C. F. Wolff tries to explain the nature of life by completely ousting the essential force [*Wesenskraft*] and the animal functions from the machine, thus creating the concept of the body without yet having the expression for it, Leibniz transforms the meaning of *mechanism* through his crossing of the frontier to the infinite into that of organism. For Wolff the word *organism* primarily means something organized, artificially ordered to serve a function—that is, something mechanical in the current sense of the word—Leibniz, on the other hand, reinterprets the machine into an entelechy, the body living out of an inner *telos.*[7]

This idea of a mechanism ensouled down to its infinitely small particles results in a fantastic vision of the living nature of matter. Down to its smallest particles, matter remains a world of creatures, entelechies, animals, living beings, souls—that is, monads. Each part of matter must be envisioned as a garden full of plants or a pond full of fishes. And every branch of the plant, every limb of every animal, every drop of its juices is another such garden or pond, on into infinity. And the air between the plants and the water between the fishes are also plant and fish, only so minute as to be imperceptible. This kind of mechanistic vitalization is the farthest point to be at-

---

7. *Ibid.,* especially §64: "Ainsi, chaque corps organique d'un vivant est une espèce de machine divine, ou d'un automate naturel, qui surpasse infiniment tous les automates artificiels. Parce qu'une machine, faite, par l'art de l'homme, n'est pas machine dans chacune de ses parties; par exemple: la dent d'une roue de laiton a des parties ou fragments, qui ne nous sont plus quelque chose d'artificiel et n'ont plus rien qui marque de la machine par rapport à l'usage où la roue était destinée. Mais les machines de la nature, c'est-à-dire les corps vivants, sont encore machines, dans leurs moindres parties jusqu'à l'infini. C'est ce qui fait la différence entre la nature et l'art, c'est-à-dire entre l'art divin et le nôtre." [Thus, every organic body of a living thing is a kind of divine machine, or natural automaton, which infinitely surpasses all the artificial automatons. Because a machine made by human art is not a machine in each of its parts; for example: the tooth of a brass wheel has parts or fragments that are no longer something artificial and possess no mark of the machine in relation to the use for which the wheel is destined. But machines of nature, that is to say, living bodies, are still machines in their least parts even to infinity. This constitutes the difference between nature and art, which is to say, between divine art and ours.]

tained by a way of thinking that tries to understand the idea of the body as an inner unity in the language of the separation of body and soul.[8]

§2. Oken *[the end of the 18th century]*

We can see how very difficult it was to overcome the situation in which the idea of the unity of the body had to be expressed in terms of a bodiless soul and a soulless body from the fact that a century after Leibniz—at the height of the Romantic philosophy of nature, when organic nature was already understood as a separate realm on a level with lifeless nature and the soul—the structure of the individual was still described in terms of Leibniz' system except that the monads were now called protozoa or infusoria. In Oken's philosophy of nature, protozoa are the elements of the organic world of which all higher animals are composed, just as for Leibniz the organism was composed of monads ruled by a principal monad. Unlike the monads, the protozoa, however, are not considered the simple substances of being as a whole but are specific organic elements. Discussing protozoa, Oken says, "I maintain (though without here being able to cite reasons) that they came into being at the creation just as universally and indelibly as earth, air, and water and that, like those elements in their sphere, they are elements in the organic world, making up the primary matter not only of animals but also of plants. . . . They can therefore in this broader sense be called the primary matter of the organic."[9] As in the case of Leibniz, this assumption of indestructible organic elements having originated in the act of the original creation results here too in a theory of the metamorphosis of the organic element. Generation is thus the formation of organic higher entities out of the protozoa; death is the dissolution

8. *Ibid.*, §66: "Il y a un monde de créatures, de vivants, d'animaux, d'entéléchies, d'âmes dans la moindre partie de la matière." [There exists a world of creatures, of living beings, of animals, of entelechies, of souls within the least part of matter.] §67: "Chaque portion de la matière peut être conçue comme un jardin plein de plantes, et comme un étang plein de poissons. Mais chaque rameau de plante, chaque membre de l'animal, chaque goutte de ses humeurs est encore un tel jardin ou un tel étang." [Each portion of matter can be conceived as a garden full of plants, and as a pond full of fish. But each branch of a plant, each member of the animal, each drop of humors is still such a garden or such a pond.] See also §§68, 69.

9. Lorenz Oken, *Die Zeugung* (1805), 22.

[Still a mechanical model, but protozoa work together in a distinct function]

of the higher unity into its elements—"a reduction of life to its primordial stage."[10] Individuals must die; still, death is not annihilation but transition to new life. "Dying is a being called back into God, in whom everything has had its origin." Individuals do not issue directly from other individuals but only via detour through God. "Though the disappearance and appearance of individuals is merely a metamorphosis of one into the other, a *transmigration of souls*, their journey goes through God."[11] Therefore, there are no preformed organisms but "only infusorial vesicles, which form different combinations of different shapes and grow into higher organisms."[12]

This idea that the individual is composed of elements and then dissolves again—that is, the idea of genesis and catagenesis as Oken understands it—has lost nothing of its mechanical character. This gives rise to the great difficulty of reinterpreting the mechanical image into the genuinely organic image of individual development. Because of the undeniably mechanical formulation, Oken cannot, of course, overcome this difficulty. Instead, with a bold intellectual stroke, he must demand that the mechanical composition not be understood as such but as something completely different, namely, as assimilating growth:

The union of protozoa in the flesh should not be pictured like a mechanical adhesion of one tiny animal to another, as in a heap of sand where the grains are not connected in any other way than simply lying next to each other— no! Analogous to the disappearance of hydrogen and oxygen in water, mercury and sulfur in cinnabar, this union is a genuine interpenetration, a growing together, a fusion of all these protozoa. From that point on they cease to lead a life of their own and, in the service of the higher organism, work toward the same shared function, or through their fusion they are this function itself. Here individuality is not respected; it simply perishes as such, and—figuratively speaking—the individualities of all protozoa now form one sole individuality—the former are annihilated, and the latter emerges only out of that annihilation.[13]

Thus, even in the Romantic era the problem of the organic was, at least in part, formulated in a very external way, for example, when

10. Lorenz Oken, *Lehrbuch der Naturphilosophie,* 2d revised ed. (Jena, 1831), §960.
11. *Ibid.,* §§904–14.
12. *Ibid.,* §961.
13. Oken, *Die Zeugung,* 23.

Oken believes that assuming the existence of organic elements would render the mechanist notion of a whole composed of preexisting parts unmechanical, because what matters for the understanding of the body as an inner unity is only the principle of this unity and that all components function as genuine members of the bodily unity. It matters very little what the members of the body do before they become members, before they are integrated into the system of the body. The body does not consist of "elements"— whether organic or inorganic—but of members of a system that are held together by one and the same organizing law of the body. In the above-cited passage, Oken must have recourse to this organizing law of the individual body as a compelling law to make the internal unity of the "elements" comprehensible. When the elements enter into the organism, they cease being elements: as elements they are annihilated—analogously to the elements that enter into a chemical combination—and even the statement that the individualities of all form only one individuality is merely figurative since the individualities of the elements have been absorbed. They have become "identical"—that is, they are subject to *one* law, which organizes them into equal members of the body's system by annihilating their previous individual autonomy. Where this organizing law comes from, however, remains as obscure in Oken as it was in Leibniz although Oken also has a counterpart to Leibniz' *entéléchie dominante*—the Graafian follicle that absorbs and forms the spermatozoa. According to Oken, the differences between species of the organic world originate in the structure of this follicle; however, this "structure" is not to be regarded as something mechanical but rather "as the type-determining force of this particular animal": "When I speak of the form of the follicle, it should not be envisioned as simply a hollow mold, into which the spermatozoa are poured. Nature does not form by embossing but penetrates the innermost part of the atom, of matter, and arranges them in their positions and orbits from the inside out, just as a magnetic flux orients iron filings in a regular pattern or as in chemistry salt solutions can be turned into crystals."[14]

Therefore the quantity of the matter added during conception does not matter at all, since the form is neither wide nor narrow—

14. *Ibid.*, 105.

"in any case, the *entire* type is stamped on what is present." There is still a lingering difference between artifact and *machine divine*, but the notion of the natural unity has already become much more inward than it was for Leibniz. The organism is a structure all members of which are ruled by a type-forming force, and its development begins with a substance that we will call here—to avoid the misunderstandings repeatedly arising from the terms *matter* and *soul*—an organic idea. It is a concrete, potent, ultimate substance, which can take in matter and reshape it in the act of absorption in accordance with its idea, reorganizing it into members of itself. In the organic idea, those two underlying realities we encountered in analyzing Ray's ideas on species are fused into one: the essence as operative cause of the phenomenon and the essence as the essentiality that is discernible for the observer in the traits that form the type. Both fuse into the idea, the idea manifest in the body and forming the type and developing into the organism as it grows, and this organism is adequately described by its typical complex of traits relevant to the essence of the being.

Body consists not of ind. elements but held . . .

Cosmology developing to look at big things — Chemistry develops to examine really small things.

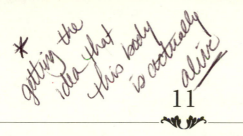

*getting the idea that this body is actually alive

11

Infinite Series and Finitization

The transition from the transcendent to the immanent view can be traced in each aspect of the life problem. In the two preceding chapters we have shown efforts to contrast the essence of a living unity with a mechanism or artifact, to point out the idea of the living body in general. We now turn to the transformation of the theory that is to explain the species characteristics of a life-form and their constancy through the generations. The pure typical case of a transcendent explanation is Linnaeus' theory, according to which God created at the beginning of the world the various animal species and endowed the individuals of each species with the ability to bring forth their own kind; in fact, the species was the quintessence of the individuals who have descended from each other through procreation; in theory the species was coined by God's creative hand. When fixity of the species was understood in this way, there was hardly any reason to look for the inner causes of the individual's character; the reference to God as the transcendent creator of the world in its thusness was sufficient. Of all the theoreticians of biology of his day, Linnaeus was most deeply immersed in the Christian worldview. Linnaeus believed that the world actually had a definite beginning; there was a day and an hour when the world, in the organization of its existence, emerged from the chaos through God's creating hand. When this belief died, the teaching of the species and its duration became questionable, leading to those transformations in the theory with which we must now concern ourselves.

When the world was no longer believed to be the creation of a higher being, the act of creation was no longer the real starting point in time of the world and its many species. The "world" was no longer a finite event that was on some level actually delimited

How are things created? ——> w/ the emergence of science —

in time by a transcendent being. And while the similarity of individuals had been understood as caused by a similar pressure of the divine hand, the theory of the fixity of the species was now also shaken. The succession of generations no longer had a finite beginning in the creation or an origin of its specific laws; instead, the succession could be traced from any individual back into infinity without this regression coming up against a point of origin for the law of the species. The result was a peculiar, undecided state. The concept of creation was replaced by the idea of infinity. Preformist theory, which envisioned the germs of all individuals contained in the first progenitors of each species—for example, the human ones in the body of Eve—had to change, and replace this real definite beginning with the series of infinite encapsulations. Now if the image of the created finite succession of generations is supplanted by the idea of an infinite succession without any real beginning, the idea that the law of this succession was created transcendentally at the beginning of the succession of generations becomes meaningless, and speculation forces us moreover to the formulation of that law in such a way that the law of the species can be directly discerned in each individual of the species. A shift of the cause of the fixity of the species to infinitely distant specimens became pointless because according to the law of the infinite succession it must be assumed that each individual was descended from a predecessor. This led to the speculative leap to the lawfulness of the species as a real cause [*Realgrund*] that is at work in all individuals of a species, thus necessarily also in the one currently under observation, without having to be traced back to preceding ones. This finitization of the law of the species in turn invalidates the idea of infinity that, for one speculative moment, served as the explanatory cause of the species—that is, for the moment when the act of creation had ceased to be the starting point of the succession of generations and it was still believed, in accord with the rationalistic encapsulation theory, that the regression to the preceding individual could explain the one descended from it. This open, undecided moment came to an end with the abolition of the idea of infinity and with the adaptation of the concept of law to the finite style of the new concept of the organism.

To clarify the biological relevance of this speculative position, I

116

[handwritten margin note:] If the laws of speciation isn't there in the first one, then the notion of an infinite thing gets thrown out the window.

will first analyze Buffon's theory, which has formulated the difficulties inherent in the concept of the infinite succession in relation to the issue of preformation. I will follow up this discussion with the fundamental formulation Leibniz gave this issue in the mathematical question of infinity.

§1. Buffon

In his four propositions Linnaeus presented the species as created all at once and then subdivided into the generations of its individuals; the *how* of this process of individuation did not seem open to question. The succession became a problem only when biological inquiry starts with the individual and finds its attempt to explain the individual caught up in the infinite regress of encapsulations of preformed germs without coming any closer to an understanding of the concrete individual in its self-contained existence. In this succession, in the continuous renewal and duration of the species, lies the mystery of nature, as Buffon argues when he attempts to fathom the nature of these succeeding generations and to elucidate the underlying problem. The ability to produce offspring of one's kind, this curious lasting, apparently eternal unity—this to Buffon was the unfathomable mystery.[1] The permanence of the species, which Linnaeus held to be the indisputable, God-created *unitas* of the series of individuals, becomes a problem for Buffon, who wants to understand the individual in its organic unity as a totality and as a totality of a specific kind. He held those creatures to be individuals of a species who perpetuate themselves through copulation and thus preserve the image of the species. Individuals who do not produce offspring of their kind when they copulate must be regarded as belonging to different species.[2] Thus, the chain of successive individual existences

---

1. Buffon, *Histoire naturelle*, Pt. 3, p. 3: "Cette faculté de produire son semblable, qui réside dans les animaux, et dans les végétaux, cette espèce d'unité toujours subsistante et qui paraît éternelle, cette vertu procréatrice qui s'exerce perpétuellement sans se détruire jamais est pour nous un mystère dont il semble qu'il ne nous est pas permis de sonder la profondeur." [This faculty of producing its likeness, which resides in the animals and in the vegetables, that kind of ever subsisting and seemingly eternal unity, that procreative virtue that is exercised perpetually without destroying itself, is a mystery for us, of which it seems that we are not permitted to sound the depths.]

2. *Ibid.*, 15: "C'est qu'on doit regarder comme la même espèce celle qui, au moyen de la copulation, ce perpétue et conserve la similitude, et comme des espèces différentes celles qui, par le même moyen, ne peuvent rien produire ensemble." [One ought to regard as the same species, whatever perpetuates itself and conserves the

Species = infinite generation
individual as a self-contained human being.

of the same species constitutes *l'existence réelle de l'espèce*.[3] The infinite succession of generations with the same species characteristics is thus identical with the species itself, and Buffon then has to wonder whether seeing the individual as a part of this succession contributes anything to an understanding of the individual as a self-contained being. Buffon answers in the negative and justifies his position by dissolving the problem of infinity.

He presents an excellent explanation of the genesis of the concept of infinity through the gradual addition of finite steps and demonstrates that the concept of infinity becomes meaningless if we keep in mind that the infinite regression is made up of finite steps. The infinite is nothing more than the finite realm with the boundaries removed; these boundaries are by nature a matter of quantity. As a result the infinite has become an intrinsically absurd concept. There is no actual infinite—that is, something infinite cannot be a subject of finite thinking.[4] Regarding the problem of species this means that the inquiry has to start with the self-contained unity of the individual, which is determined by its species. Several such unities of the same species form a finite series or succession, and from here theory (at any rate the preformation theory) makes the leap of attempting to explain the nature of the species on the basis of the infinite succession. However, according to Buffon, this infinity

similarity by means of copulation, and as different species whatever cannot produce anything similar by the same means.]

3. *Ibid.*, 25: "Cette chaine d'existences successives d'individus, qui constitue l'existence réelle de l'espèce" [that chain of successive individual existences, which constitutes the real existence of the species].

4. *Ibid.*, 38: "L'idée de l'infini ne peut venir que de l'idee du fini, c'est ici un infini de succession, un infini géometrique, chaque individu est une unité, plusieurs individus font un nombre fini, et l'espèce est le nombre infini; ainsi de la même façon que l'on peut démontrer que l'infini géométrique n'existe point, on s'assurera que le progrès ou le développement à l'infini n'existe point non plus; que ce n'est qu'une idée d'abstraction un retranchement à l'idée du fini, auquel on ôte les limites qui doivent nécessairement terminer toute grandeur, et que par conséquent on doit rejeter de la Philosophie toute opinion qui conduit nécessairement à l'idée de l'existence actuelle de l'infini géometrique ou arithmétique." [The idea of the infinite can only come from the idea of the finite, in this case an infinity of succession, a geometric infinity, each individual is a unity, many individuals constitute a finite number, and the species is the infinite number; and so in the same manner that one can demonstrate that the geometric infinity does not exist, one will be assured that progress or development to infinity also has no existence; that this is nothing more than an idea produced by abstraction, a deduction from the idea of the finite, in which one removes the limits that should bound any magnitude, and that as a consequence one ought to reject from philosophy every opinion which leads necessarily to the idea of the actual existence of geometric or arithmetic infinity.]

does not really exist; it is no *existence actuelle* but an abstraction. By nature extension is finite; to assume an actually infinite extension is a contradiction in terms. Those who nevertheless make such an assumption, according to Buffon, have to confine themselves to saying that the *infini de successions et de multiplications* is nothing more than an extension with an indefinite upper limit—not an *infini* but an *indéfini*.[5] Pointing out the infinite divisibility of matter also does not hold good; rather this argument must be countered with the point that the same illusions connected with the infinite divisibility are also associated with all other kinds of mathematical infinity: these infinities do not exist in actual fact but are merely intellectual abstractions.[6] Therefore, dissolving the species into an infinite regression is not a sufficient answer to the question of how we are to understand the nature and reproduction of life-forms.[7]

We can understand Buffon's reasoning only if we assume a complete breakdown of the idea Linnaeus had still considered valid, namely, that of a finite, self-contained world created by God. In this self-contained worldview, the creation of the species unit by God is a completely adequate explanation of the species characteristics of the individual. It is only when the rampartlike boundaries of this world are breached and the succession of generations extends into infinity that the problem of actual infinity becomes discernible in a meaningful way. It is only when the dogmatic framework breaks down and the empirical stance attempts to understand the isolated individual in its particularity that the problem Buffon presents arises.

§2. Leibniz

At the end of the chapter of Buffon's *Histoire naturelle* (p. 250) that contains the investigations of the problem of infinite we find the

---

5. *Ibid.*, 39.
6. *Ibid.*, 234: "Mais je réponds qu'on se fait sur cette divisibilité à l'infini la même illusion que sur toutes les autres espèces d'infinis géometriques ou arithméthiques: ces infinis ne sont tous que des abstractions de notre esprit, et n'existent pas dans la nature des choses." [But I answer that one makes the same illusion about the divisibility into infinity as about all the other types of geometric or arithmetic infinities: all these infinities are nothing but abstractions of our minds, and do not exist in the nature of things.]
7. *Ibid.*, 40.

date February 6, 1746; the volume was published in 1750. For further details concerning his ideas, Buffon refers the reader to the foreword of his translation of Newton (not available to me),[8] which appeared in 1740, and thus to the larger mathematical context of the problems associated with the analysis of infinity in his time. The most significant and most concise fundamental formulations of the problem are found in some letters from Leibniz to Bernoulli (published in 1745). For our purposes the letter of July 29, 1698, is especially important because it contains a statement referring to the problem of preformation. There Leibniz speaks about the division of matter, arguing that no indivisible elements or smallest particles can ever be arrived at, only ever smaller ones that can be split into yet smaller ones. By the same token, increasing a dimension will never lead to the largest one or to infinitely large ones or to ones whose dimensions cannot be increased further. Applying these principles to the problem of preformation, Leibniz concedes that the germs may be encapsulated but denies that it is possible to arrive at an infinitely small one, much less at an ultimate one.[9] The regression of encapsulation is thus extended into infinity, and the act of creation loses its significance as an absolute beginning. Another passage in a letter of August, 1698, shows even more clearly that in the infinite regression for each member we must necessarily envision another one, and thus the concept of an absolute infinity is a contradiction in terms. The passage is formulated with particular felicity because it distinctly shows the connection between the problem of the infinitely large with that

8. *Ibid.*, 38ff. refers to pp. 7–8 of the foreword of his translation of Newton. The citation of the title is incomplete. According to the catalogue of the Bibliothèque Nationale, the full title of the work is: Newton, *La Méthode des fluxions et des suites infinies* (Paris, 1740).

9. Leibniz to Bernoulli, July 29, 1698: "Etsi enim concedam, nullam esse portionem materiae, quae non actu sit secta, non tamen ideo devenitur ad elementa insecabilia aut ad minimas portiones, immo nec ad infinite parvas, sed tantum ad minores perpetuo at tamen ordinarias; similiter ut ad majores perpetuo in augendo acceditur. Sic etiam semper animalcula in animalculis dari facile concedo; et tamen necesse non est dari animalcula infinite parva, nedum ultima." [For although I concede that there is no portion of matter that is not divided, one does not therefore arrive thereby at indivisible elements or at minimal portions, nay more, even at infinitely small ones, but only at perpetually smaller yet nevertheless ordinary ones; similarly, as one attains to perpetually larger ones by augmentation. So also I easily concede that minute animals exist within small animals; and yet there is no necessity that there exists an infinitely small animal, nor even a last one.]

of the infinitely small; from the vantage point of empirical finite facts, speculation on infinity leads to meaninglessness in both directions.[10]

10. August, 1698: "Cum negavi, ad minimas portiones deveniri, facile judicari poterat, me non locutum de nostris divisionibus, sed etiam de illis, quae actu fiunt in natura. Etsi igitur pro certo habeam, quamlibet partem materiae esse rursus actu subdivisam, non ideo tamen hinc sequi puto, quod detar portio materiae infinite parva, et minus adhuc sequi concedo, quod ulla detur portio omnino minima. Si quis consecutionem in formam redigere velit, sentiet difficultatem. *At inquies: Si nulla est infinite exigua, ergo singulae sunt finitae* (concedo); *si singulae sunt finitae, ergo omnes simul sumptae constituent magnitudinem infinitam.* Hanc consequentiam non concedo; concederem si aliqua daretur finita, quae minor esset ceteris omnibus vel certe nulla alia major; tunc enim fateor talibus assumptis, pluribus quam est datus numerus quivis, oriri quantitatem, majorem data quavis. Sed constat, quavis parte aliam minorem finitam dari." [Since I have denied arriving at minimal portions, it was easy to judge that I was not speaking of our divisions, but also about those actually occurring in nature. Therefore, although I certainly hold that any part of matter whatsoever is actually subdivided again, still I do not think it therefore follows from this that there exists an infinitely small portion of matter, and still less do I concede that it follows that there exists any altogether minimal portion. If anyone wishes to pursue the consequence formally, he will sense the difficulty. *But you will inquire: If nothing infinitely small exists, then single parts are finite* (I concede); *if singular parts are finite, therefore all taken together at once constitute an infinite magnitude.* I do not concede this conclusion. I would concede, if there existed some finitude which would be smaller than all others or certainly not greater than any other; for then I confess that on such assumptions, by as many as any given number you like there arises a quantity as large as you like. But it holds true that by any part you like another smaller finite magnitude exists.]

The problem of the given fact of an actual infinite again plays an important role in the history of modern mathematics, especially in the construction of Cantor's set theory and theory of transfinite cardinal numbers, sets of sets, and so forth. This development in mathematics is essentially based on the same false reasoning Leibniz discussed in his letters to Bernoulli and Buffon addressed in the context of his criticism of the theory of preformation. Lately Felix Kaufmann has tried in his works to resolve this false reasoning of set theory and the mathematical theory based on it. His argumentation is essentially the same as Buffon's, cited earlier in the text. I quote from Kaufmann's book, *Das Unendliche in der Mathematik und seine Ausschaltung* (Vienna, 1930), 147: "We have established that the natural numbers are logical abstracts of the counting process and that the concept of the 'number series' includes an 'idealization' in addition to this abstraction. It consists of the presupposition of the nonexistence of a fixed upper limit, so that 'number series' comes to mean the abstraction of an infinite counting process." He points out that we must avoid the error "of seeing a self-contained totality of natural numbers in the number series" (148). We must start with the counting process and determine its logical structure; the series of natural numbers must be defined by the law of their formation and not conversely the general form of the process by its product, assumed to be real. In his "Bemerkungen zum Grundlagenstreit in Logik und Mathematik" (*Erkenntnis*, II, 1931) Kaufmann summarized the problem most concisely in the sentence (285): "The *circularity* (namely, of the concept of the infinite series of natural numbers) lies in the fact that in general where no final limit exists for the number of the function values, the value trend [*Wertverlauf*] of a function can be defined only as a general form, and therefore it is not possible to define this general form by the value trend."

12

Inner Form and Formative Drive

Something about these things that run themselves — [handwritten]

§1. Inner Form (Buffon)

what interior our mold?. [handwritten, left margin]

If we avoid the error of speculation on infinity, that is, of seeing a given whole in the succession of individuals of a species, we have to deal with the question that also arises when the problem of the organism is shifted back into the "animal in itself," namely, the question of the individual organism's unity as it is defined by its species. To answer it, Buffon developed the theory of the *moule intérieur*, the internal form of the organism. Just as we humans can make forms that mold the exterior of things, so we must conclude, according to Buffon, that nature can create forms to give things not only their external shapes but also their internal ones. This contrast of human external and natural internal shape recalls Leibniz' antithesis of human and divine machine. And Buffon also develops his idea further along the lines of Leibniz' *machine divine* when he defines the animal body as a kind of internal form in which the substances that serve growth are shaped and assimilated to the whole.[1] The entire

---

1. Buffon, *Histoire naturelle*, Pt. 3, p. 60: "Le corps d'un animal est une espèce de moule intérieur, dans lequel la matière qui sert à son accroissement se modèle et s'assimile au total; de manière que sans qu'il arrive aucun changement à l'ordre et à la proportion des parties, il en résulte cependant une augmentation dans chaque partie prise séparément." [The animal's body is a kind of interior mold, in which the matter that effects growth is modeled and assimilated to the whole, in a manner that, without undergoing any change of the order and proportion of the parts, there results in the meantime an augmentation in each part taken separately.] It should be noted that Buffon does not speak of the inner form as an entity located *in* the body and functioning as its building principle; rather body and inner form are seen as identical. This formulation is so radical that it comes close to creating the concept of the spiritual body.

For an illustration of this by analogy to inorganic forces, see also Buffon, *Histoire naturelle*, Pt. 3, p. 51: "Ces moules intérieurs, que nous n'aurons jamais, la Nature peut les avoir, car elle a les qualités de la pesanteur, qui en effet pénètre à l'interieur." [These molds, that we never have, nature can have, for it has the qualities of gravity, which has the effect of penetrating to the interior.] Compare also the above-cited passage from Oken, *Zeugung*, 97.

By what are you declaring these 2 things similar to be similar by... [handwritten]

body is animated by the same organizing principle, down to its smallest particle; each member of the body is still such a *moule intérieur* through which the growth of the entire organism is shaped proportionately. Thus, no part is subject to a mechanical accumulation of matter; rather, each part organizes the nutrients it receives in the way and to the extent appropriate for it. The inner form is a *qualité intérieure*, a *puissance active*, a *force pénétrante*—all terms meant to express the complete penetration of the organism by this organic force. To facilitate his readers' understanding, Buffon recalls analogies to inorganic forces: weight, *les attractions magnétiques*, *les affinités chymiques*, which govern the bodies subject to them in every particle. These efforts to make the penetration of the organism by its organizing principle comprehensible parallel later attempts to explain the nature of the social totality with analogies to the organism. In his day Buffon could expect his readers to be sufficiently familiar with the magnetic, chemical, and gravitational phenomena so he could use them as effective images, just as in the nineteenth century people had become used to thinking of the organism, which could be used to support a theory of society in order to substantiate that the whole is inherent in each of its members. For Buffon, *pesanteur* was a quality permeating the mass *dans les parties les plus intimes*, and the inner permeating forms had to be understood analogously.[2]

§2. The Formative Drive (Blumenbach)

The theory of the inner form entered the German thinking about the organism by way of Blumenbach's theory of the formative drive [*Bildungstrieb*]. Like Buffon, Blumenbach opposed the theory of preformed forms and was convinced of the inadequacy of the creation theory. He believed—and therefore called himself an epigeneticist—"that in the previously raw, unformed seminal matter of the

---

2. Buffon's theory of how these *moules intérieurs* come about, his theory of procreation, is of interest to us only because it shows the state of biological theory that was also still valid for Darwin. In Buffon's opinion, the inner forms are produced from the surplus nourishment of the body parts; those assimilated parts of nutrients that are not used for the organism's further expansion after growth has been completed, accumulate in the seminal fluid in such a way that this is a true copy of the entire body in miniature (since it is gathered from all the parts of the body). Darwin again constructed a similar theory of the creation of the germ cells from all parts of the organism; he called it the theory of pangenesis.

123

organized body, after it has matured and has arrived at its destination in the body a special drive then becomes active and will continue to be active throughout the creature's life. This drive at first prompts the organism to take on its proper form, which it then maintains for the rest of its life and which it restores, if possible, if the organism is ever mutilated." This drive belongs to the vital forces in general but differs clearly from the specialized powers of the organic body—contractibility, irritability, sensibility—and from the general physical forces in that it is "the first and most important force for all production, nourishment, and reproduction." To distinguish it from other vital forces, it could be "given the name formative drive (*nisus formativus*)." Like Buffon, Blumenbach compares the formative drive to gravity and the force of attraction, both of which we cannot comprehend but can nevertheless assume to exist because of their effects, which we can observe. The term *formative drive,* too, is intended solely to "designate a force whose constant effect must be acknowledged based on experience but whose *cause,* like that of the above-mentioned generally acknowledged natural forces, is a *qualitas occulta* for us."[3]

The term *drive* marks an essential step toward the internalization of the idea of the body, something Blumenbach's great contemporaries clearly recognized and welcomed. Concepts such as essential force [*Wesenskraft*] (Wolff) and Buffon's forms still had to struggle with static or mechanical notions, whether those of mechanical and chemical natural forces or that of the "external" form. The drive, on the other hand, shifts the form-giving principle to inside the organism and at the same time portends something of the subjectivity of reproduction. Goethe considered just this nuance of Blumenbach's concept especially important and stressed his preference for this term over the others, which still left something to be desired, "for something material always clings to any organic matter, no matter how alive we envision it to be. The word *force* basically designates something purely physical, even mechanical, and what is to emerge out of this matter remains an obscure, incomprehensible point to us. Now Blumenbach achieved the highest and ultimate meaning of the expression: he anthropomorphized the word of the enigma and named the topic under discussion a *nisus formati-*

3. Johann Friedrich Blumenbach, *Über den Bildungstrieb* (Göttingen, 1791).

"can't find it – so it's not there"

all started from
somewhere –

vus, a drive, a vigorous activity through which formation is to be effected." The anthropomorphic content of the drive was so attractive to Goethe that he pursued it further and—like Schelling at a later time—drew the conclusion "that, in order to examine what is at hand, we must admit an antecedent activity, and that, if we want to envision this activity, we must assign to it a fitting element on which it can work, and that, finally, we must think of this activity with this material as always existing together and eternally present together at the same time. We encounter this awesome activity in its personification as a god, a creator, and preserver, whom we are called upon to worship, venerate, and praise in every way."[4]

Goethe returned to Blumenbach's work, which he had read earlier without fully taking it in, because Kant expressed his appreciation for the concept of the formative drive in his *Critique of Judgment.* However, Kant's praise was aimed in a direction diametrically opposed to Goethe's interest. While Goethe was attracted by the subjectivization of nature, Kant thought the theory of the formative drive could preserve the general natural lawfulness against the exaggerated, "hyperphysical," teleological interpretations of the products of nature. Kant—like Buffon before him—saw the preformation theory as merely an attempt to shift the occasionalism of procreation back to the beginning of the world, with divine art not intervening directly in each act of procreation but having created the entire diversity of the organic world all at once, "as if it were not all the same whether such forms had their supernatural origin at the beginning of the world or in its continuation."[5] The epigenetic theory, on the other hand, leaves the field to nature, at least in respect to reproduction, in matters that originally could be grasped only in terms of the causality of purpose; thus it works with the least involvement of the supernatural since it leaves everything except the beginning of the world to nature, "though without determining anything about this first beginning, which all of physics fails to explain regardless of what chain of causes it employs in its attempts at an explanation."[6]

In spite of their different interpretations, Goethe and Kant agree

4. Goethe, "Bildungstrieb," in *Naturwissenschaft im Allgemeinen.*
5. Immanuel Kant, *Kritik der Urteilskraft,* §81, p. 377 (quoted from the edition of Philosophische Bibliothek, Meiner; page numbers in the original edition).
6. *Ibid.,* 378.

in the effort once and for all to delimit the sphere of the organic from all adjacent ones. When Goethe interprets—even overinterprets—the concept of the formative drive by emphasizing its anthropomorphic content, the closeness to the human sphere is not intended to lead to a blending of the two but merely to more clearly differentiate the living from the mechanical. On the other hand, when Kant extends the meaning of the concept toward nature, here understood as also encompassing the inorganic realm, he does not mean to abolish the distinction between organism and mechanism but intends only to preserve the uniqueness of the self-contained organism as a unity against hyperphysical theories of intervention of an architectonic intellect at arbitrary points in natural events. At the intersection of both interpretations, each of which somewhat overshoots the mark, we find the idea of the organism, finally balanced out.

Being by itself, internally, run by itself, internally, (not by God) so we just have to find what's running it.

13

The Concept of the Organism in the
Critique of Judgment

In intellectual history [*der Bewegung des Geistes*] the *Critique of Judgment* is where the concept of the organism finds itself in balance. Kant struggled to understand the organism, as we have seen, by excluding it from the sphere of a creating reason. This intention is typified in the passage cited above, in which Kant opposed the preformation theory by arguing that it does not matter at all whether one assumes only one occasion or numerous instances of divine intervention as an explanation of nature and its processes. Thus Kant rejects both forms of creationist theory. This is a complete reversal of the line of argument Kant used in the *Critique of Pure Reason* in his explication of the Third Antinomy to justify the parallelism of the natural and the intelligible spheres. In his note to the thesis that in an explanation of phenomena in the world freedom must be considered as a cause, Kant proceeds from positing such a free cause as an explanation of the origin of the world to the conclusion that at any point in the course of the world spontaneous acts of freedom can possibly set in motion new lines of natural events. According to Kant, for the purposes of this argument the question of how such an intervention from outside is possible can remain unanswered since we do not even know how things work within nature.

Just as this argument served in the *Critique of Pure Reason* to maintain man's spontaneity out of pure reason against the course of lawful nature, so it can now in its reversal serve to protect natural processes and their inherent laws against spontaneous, foreign interventions. Kant excludes not only occasional interventions at arbitrary points but also the single creation of living nature through an original creative act—although we are then confronted by the problem of an absolute beginning of sequences of events, a problem Kant did not neglect to mention. If this argument had been intended to

Kant denies divine intervention

This thing has to be self-contained in itself

you can't understand how the parts go together if you don't know what the whole is —

push the organism back into the mechanical processes of nature, the entire second part of the *Critique of Judgment* would have been superfluous. However, it is not superfluous because certain natural products, the so-called natural purposes [*Naturzwecke*], emerge as undisputed facts from the lawful processes of nature. The existence of the organic as a primary phenomenon precedes all philosophical interpretations of it. According to Kant, the organic is defined by three factors: (1) organic beings reproduce themselves as beings of a genus through procreation; (2) they produce themselves as individual beings through their ability to grow by assimilating inorganic substances; (3) as whole beings, they are produced by their parts in such a way that the preservation of the whole depends on the preservation of the parts, and vice versa. Because of these facts preceding speculation and characterized in this way, these "beings organized as natural purpose" must be investigated scientifically in accordance with the mechanical laws of nature and must also be interpreted as purposes—in particular, as natural purposes—that is, as beings that function alternately as cause and as effect for themselves. The connection among the operative causes within them must also be able to be seen as a connection by way of final causes.

We are already familiar with the difficulties in rationally explaining the unity of the organism on the levels of mechanical causes and categories of purposes. In Kant's view, for a thing to be a natural purpose, the parts must depend on their relationship to the whole for their existence. However, if this were the only defining criterion then the whole of nature would be an artificial product, split into plan and parts. If the natural product is to be able to exist without a relationship to a rationally planning and constructing being outside it, then the parts must connect with each other in such a way that they are alternately cause and effect of their form. For only then, Kant reasons, can the idea of the whole once again determine the form and interconnection of all parts, "not as cause—for then it would be an artificial product—but as the foundation for an understanding of the systematic unity and interconnection of the diversity contained in the matter at hand for the observer."[1]

The characterization of the member of the organism as related to every other member of the whole and thereby to the whole itself,

1. Immanuel Kant, *Kritik der Urteilskraft*, §65, p. 291.

128

that is, as an expression of the total organism, is much more precise and clearer than all earlier ones. Based on the clarity of this view, Kant succeeds in establishing the meaning of the concept of the organ that is for us now the only one—that of the organ as a member of the living organism, in contrast to the earlier concept of the organ as a tool. For instance, Kant writes:

In such a product of nature, every part not only exists *by means* of all the other parts but also exists *for the sake of* the others and the whole—that is, as an (organ) instrument. But this is not enough (since it could also be a man-made instrument and thus could only exist at all as a purpose); instead, as an organ that *produces* the other parts (all of them mutually producing one another), it cannot be a man-made instrument but only one of nature, which supplies all the material for instruments (even for man-made ones). Only then and only for that reason can such a product as an organized and self-organizing being "be called a natural purpose."[2]

Here the meaning of Leibniz' concept of the *machine divine* is established as precisely as possible as a product of nature, ruled by an inwardly formative force; a machine, on the other hand, is defined as having only a moving force. What this formative force is can be understood only approximately, by analogy—by the thoroughly explicated analogy of the artifact and through the "analogon of life." For Kant, life is identical not with the organic but with the rational soul—and therefore, "strictly speaking, the organization of nature is not analogous to any causality we know." The organism is neither artifact nor soul but rather the third, fully autonomous element, the nature of which we can discuss only in metaphors and which we must accept as a primary mode of being, just like matter and soul. The dualism of soulless matter and of life as a soul without substance has not yet been resolved, but the central form of the body—which is what we now mean when we speak of life, is unequivocally defined by its equal distance from these two familiar poles.

In spite of the difficulties of dealing with the phenomenon of the living body appropriately in language, it was nevertheless a phenomenon very clearly perceptible to the senses as we can see in the fact that it serves already in the *Critique of Judgment* as the point of departure for inferences by analogy to other areas of experience. Though the organism cannot be explained by the analogon of the ar-

2. *Ibid.*, 291–92.

tifact or of life, it can nevertheless "in turn shed light upon a certain union, found more as an idea than as a reality, through analogy to the already mentioned direct natural purposes. Thus, on the occasion of the recent total transformation of a great people into a state, the word *organization* was very appropriately used for the establishment of magistracies, etc., and even in reference to the whole state. For of course in such a whole each member should not only be a means but also a purpose, and by contributing to making the whole possible, each member's position and function should also be determined by the idea of the whole."[3]

Similarly, the concept of the formative drive, so painstakingly developed, served already then to clarify societal phenomena. In 1790 Friedrich Jacobi noted in a letter, "That none of all of our constitutions can last much longer—of that I am convinced because almost nothing is left of their original *formative drive*. King—nobility—the clergy—nothing but hollow masks—dried-up bones. Who can say what will happen, or at least say what should happen? I think, I mull it over—and fall silent."[4]

---

3. *Ibid.*, 294, note. At the same time, however, in Herder: "And in both cases it [the state] will aspire to the highest model of an animate machine, the human body itself" (1788). Herder, *Sämmtliche Werke,* ed. Bernhard Suphan (Berlin, 1877–1913), XVI, 601: "Idee zum ersten patriotischen Institut für den Allgemeingeist Deutschlands."
4. *Friedrich Heinrich Jacobis Werke,* III (Leipzig, 1816), p. 537. Letter to Julia, Countess R——, Pempelfort, November 5, 1790.

max Weber —
" organization "
a life of its own ...
long after you retire

Retirement —
amputated from the
organism

14

The Unfolding of
the World of Organic Forms

The idea of the living individual being gradually gains ground and becomes clearer until it becomes so vivid and expressive that it in turn becomes a fixed term in the comparative definition of social subjects. We cannot distinguish what is cause and effect, but in this development of the metaphor the direct experience of the living being as a self-contained being that matures according to its inherent formative law combines strangely with the speculations on the problem of infinity, which are forced on the observer as a result of the collapse of the creationist worldview. In addition, the same experience and the same speculation that produced the image of the living individual now push people to a new perspective on the whole living world. The Linnaean theses have completely lost their interpretive power. When the creation as an act at a definite point in time disappeared, the explanation of the individual on the basis of the *unitas* of the created species and the interpretation of the entire living world as a diversity of forms created at one time both also disappeared. Just as the finite created species is replaced by the speculation on the infinite succession and the resulting idea of a formative principle that constantly realizes itself, so the notion of rigidly defined species arranged side by side is replaced—first cautiously, then more explicitly—by the idea of a history of the organic world. The transcendent idea of the creation is replaced with the immanent idea of history.

The process of reinterpretation cannot be traced as easily as the corresponding process that led to the development of the idea of the organism because the intellectual threads going from one idea to the other are more numerous and more intertwined. We find intertwined here the following: (1) the logical idea of a continuity of forms—the idea that the diversity of organic forms actually repre-

what is woman composed of? You actually did come from your predecessor

sents a continuum akin to the mathematical one, or at least that it could be considered as such; (2) the idea of a morphological kinship among life forms—the idea that the diversity of forms can be classified according to proximity and distance, rich or stunted development in regard to a shared blueprint; (3) the ontological speculation on the nature of the organic levels of existence (plant, animal, man) is also mixed in; and finally (4) the idea of a real descent of various life-forms from each other is also added.

We will attempt to cut through this web of ideas in such a way that the change from the transcendent to the immanent view of the world of forms will become as clear as possible. To that end we discuss its aspects in the following sequence: (1) We will begin with the interpretation of the world of forms as a real continuum of reason; this interpretation is transcendent because the actual connection between the living forms is not seen residing in the unique character of a living substance but in that of a different substance, namely, the substance of reason. (2) Second, we go on to the interpretation of this connection that sees the world of forms governed by a regulative idea of the continuum. It coincides with the first interpretation in positing reason as the source of the continuum, and it takes transcendence even further than the first one in seeing *ratio* not as actually connecting the diversity of forms but as an ordering idea brought to bear on the world of forms by an observing subject. Nevertheless, this interpretation prepares the ground for the immanent interpretations insofar as the character of the continuum as a regulative idea leaves open the question of the real connection between the multifarious forms. In other words, it leaves an empty place in the interpretation of the phenomenon that can then be filled by ideas of immanence. (3) We will first answer the question—left open by the regulative idea—of the actual connection between forms through morphological studies of similarities in the blueprint, studies that allow us to categorize the world of forms on the basis of its own structure but that leave the question of the real foundation for any relatedness among forms either unanswered or answer it by referring to a transcendent power (God, nature). (4) Finally, the idea of an inner structural relatedness among forms is followed by the radically immanent idea of a real kinship among forms, according to which they have in fact developed from each other in a historical process.

Marx: People becoming parts of the whole

Reason is continual.

§1. The Diversity of Living Forms as a Real Continuum of Reason (Leibniz)

Leibniz' application of the mathematical continuity principle to organisms is probably the clearest example of a transcendental interpretation of the first type. In a letter to Varignon, Leibniz proceeds from an analysis of the geometrical continuum to the algebraic one, asserting that an equation that precisely expresses a particular condition also represents all others that can befit the same object. Then, passing on to physics, Leibniz sets up the principle that the future lies in the womb of the present and that there is consequently no room for chance. Leibniz then formulates what later became known as the Kant-Laplace universal formula: if, thanks to the formula of a higher character, it were possible to express an essential feature of the universe, then all resulting conditions for all parts of the universe and for any given time could be gathered from it.[1] From here, Leibniz takes the step to biology, and on the basis of the continuity principle he asserts that all the classes of beings that we know as different from each other are the coordinates of a curve in God's mind.

The unity of this curve does not allow that any other coordinates except the actually existing ones are inserted between any two coordinates on the curve. For inserting anything else would be a sign of disorder and incompleteness. Thus men are closely related to animals, animals to plants, and these in turn to fossils, while these latter for their part are connected with the bodies we perceive with our senses. According to the law of continuity, when the essential elements of one being come close to those of another, then all other characteristics of the former must necessarily also steadily come closer to those of the latter. Thus, all orders of natural beings necessarily form one continuous chain, in which the various classes, like so many rings, are so closely intertwined that our senses and imagination cannot determine the precise point where one class begins and the other ends. For the borderline species—that is, all those species that, as it were, lie around the turning points and intersections, must allow a dual interpretation and be characterized by traits that can with equal justification be attributed to one or the other of the neighboring species. — Accordingly, zoophytes or, as Hudde calls them, *plant animals* are not monstrosities; rather their existence is completely in line with the order of nature. I am so convinced of the cogent force of the continuity principle that I would not be in the least sur-

---

1. Gottfried Wilhelm Leibniz, "Über das Kontinuitätsprinzip" (from a letter to Varignon), *Hauptschriften zur Grundlegung der Philosophie*, I (Philosophische Bibliothek), 75–76.

prised at the discovery of intermediate beings that in some of their traits—
perhaps in their diet and reproduction—could with equal justification be
considered plants and animals and that thus overturn the usual rules that
are based on the supposition that the various orders of beings existing in the
universe at the same time are completely and absolutely separate from each
other. Yes, I repeat, not only would I not be surprised at their existence, but
I am indeed convinced that such beings must exist and that natural history
will probably succeed some day in finding them when it begins to study in
more detail the infinite number of living beings that escape ordinary study
because they are so small or are hidden in the interior of the earth and in the
depths of the waters. We have only just begun our observations; what right
have we to dispute the findings of reason just because we have not yet had
the opportunity to observe them? The principle of continuity is thus beyond all doubt for me, and it might well serve to explain a number of important truths of that genuine philosophy that rises above the senses and the
imagination and looks for the origin of phenomena in the intellectual
sphere. I flatter myself that I have some ideas of such a philosophy, but the
century is not yet ready to accept them.[2]

The final sentences in this passage leave no doubt that Leibniz
intended the continuity of forms in the sense of a metaphysics of
reason. The origin of the organic phenomena, in all their diversity,
lies not in themselves but in the intellectual sphere. The connection between classes is not an actual physical one, not an immanent
one, but rather a transcendent one by virtue of its subordination
to the formal principle of the continuity of the whole universe
[*Weltzusammenhang*].

If in interpreting Leibniz' ideas we speak of a transcendence of
the cause compared to what is caused, we have to understand this
correctly for our speculations. The principle of continuity embodies
the idea of transcendence insofar as the sphere of the body is distinct
from that of the formal principles; in this sense the intellectual principle is transcendent in relation to the organic mode of being. Put
differently, this theory is still an *objective, realistic* interpretation
of living phenomena; the continuity principle is not a regulative
idea brought to bear upon reality by a subjective reason; rather, the
world of forms is believed to be actually continuous in God's idea.
Though the continuum cannot always be shown empirically, it exists as a metaphysical reality. Thus, it is not a matter of merely con-
sidering an actually discontinuous sequence as a continuum; rather

2. *Ibid.*, 77.

the continuity is the inner law of this sequence. And for *this* reason
Leibniz can anticipate, as a result of his theory of continuity, a
breakdown in the prevailing theory of the fixity of the species—a
breakdown, however, his century is "not yet ready" to accept. The
idea of the real continuum as it is developed by Leibniz anticipates
the dissolution of the creationist doctrine of the fixity of the species
and prepares the ground for the idea of the variation of organic
forms.

Something is happening over + over again over + above the individual.

§2. The Diversity of Living Forms Under the Regulative Idea of the Continuum (Kant)

We must fully understand the content of this idea to understand
how Kant has changed it. Kant, too, set up a law of the "continuity of
forms,"[3] but he means by that term not the real constitution of the
living world but the regulative idea of reason that controls how the
intellect deals with the diversity of forms. Continuity is a transcendental principle of reason that can be traced back to the two other
principles of homogeneity and specification. The principle of homogeneity leads us to look for similarities in diversity, and in this process we come to ever more extensive species and genera. The other
principle directs us not to take any one homogeneous group as the
final one but to look for new speciation and new diversity. Thus, no
species is the lowest, but each has to comprise more and more subspecies within itself. The principle of continuity "arises from the
union of these other two, inasmuch as only by ascending to higher
genera as well as by descending to lower species do we complete the
system's interconnectedness in the idea. For only then do all diverse
forms emerge as related, because all of them, through all gradations
of extended definitions, are descended from a sole highest genus."[4]
While these principles are not derived from experience, they are
nevertheless not the logical rules of the formation of genera and species. Instead, they are transcendental ideas that presuppose a necessary homogeneity in the diversity of nature, because "without this
there could be no empirical concepts and therefore no experience."[5]

3. Kant, *Kritik der reinen Vernunft*, B686.
4. *Ibid.*
5. *Ibid.*, B682.

The principle of continuity accordingly states that "all species in their diversity are contiguous and it is not possible to make the transition from one to another in a leap. Rather, only a gradual transition through ever smaller gradations of differences is possible between species. In other words, there are no species or subspecies that (in terms of concepts of reason) are directly adjacent to each other; there are always intermediate species possible that are less different from those two species than those latter are from each other."[6]

In transcendental philosophy, the continuity of forms is a regulative idea of reason, not a constitutive principle of the experience of nature. Its transcendent character emerges more clearly than it does in Leibniz' philosophy, in which the *ratio*, the *metaphysicum*, was the real content of things. With this turn to a stronger emphasis on the transcendence of the principle, Kant made room for the development of the world of forms in accordance with its inner law. If the idea transcending the body [*leibjenseitig*] is not seen [*subintelle-giert*] as the real ground of organic development, the way is open to adequate treatment of this development itself. Kant was well aware of the difference between his position and that of Leibniz. He discusses Leibniz' continuous ladder of creatures as merely "obeying the principle of affinity, which is based on the interest of reason."[7] Empirical observations cannot give rise to the supposition of the ladder since the rungs of such a ladder, as presented to us by experience, are spaced much too far apart; and the supposedly small differences between them are such wide gaps in nature that no continuous image can emerge.[8] Thus continuity is merely an idea, for which experience does not provide a congruent object, not only "because the species in nature are really separate from each other and must therefore constitute a *quantum discretum*," but also because this law is of no use for empirical classification since it does not provide any criteria for forming the elements of the continuum.[9] The delimitation of the units, Kant points out, is in the concrete case an expression of the particular predominant interest either in the variety based on the principle of specification, or in the unit based on the principle of aggregation in larger groups. Kant summarizes the sense

6. *Ibid.*, B687–88.
7. *Ibid.*, B696.
8. *Ibid.*
9. *Ibid.*, B695.

of this transcendent idea in a few statements every advocate of race theory ought to hang over his desk so that he can look at them every time he feels the desire to draw non sequiturs from his concept of race types or from the opposite concept of the essential sameness of all human beings for the realm of the societal spirit. Those statements are as follows:

When I see intelligent men arguing about the characteristics of humans, animals, or plants—and even of bodies in the mineral realm—because some assume, for instance, that there is a special national character due to one's descent or that there are definite, heritable differences between families, races, etc., whereas others insist that in this regard nature has given everyone the same predispositions and that all differences are solely due to external contingencies, I need only consider the nature of the matter under discussion to realize that it is too profoundly hidden a subject for either of the two parties to be talking out of insight into the nature of the matter. Their argument shows nothing more than the twofold interest of reason, of which each party takes one side to heart, or at any rate affects to do so, namely the differences between the maxims of natural diversity or of natural unity. They can very well be reconciled, but as long as they are mistaken for objective insights, they create not only arguments but also obstacles, which will block the truth for a long time until a way is found to reconcile the disputing interests and to satisfy reason on this matter.[10]

§3. The Transcendent Factual Order of the Series (Herder, Goethe)

Thanks to Kant's critique, the principle of continuity was unequivocally transformed from a real principle of nature into a transcendental idea of reason. As such, it is no longer important for the *real* interconnections in the world of organic forms. The fact that continuity, which in Leibniz was still intended as a basic framework of bodily development though itself not part of the body [*leibfremd*], so plainly revealed its transcendental character shows that the image of the internal lawfulness of this development was changing toward the idea of immanence. Herder and Goethe proposed images of development that are considerably "more inward" than those of Leibniz, even though they also do not yet entirely see development as the inner law of the organic world. The image has become more inward in that a factual [*sachhaltig*] principle of the formation of series has

10. *Ibid.*

replaced the purely formal principle of continuity; the idea of immanence has not yet been completely reached insofar as the factual principle is still conceived of as a transcendent one, as the active hand of nature or a creator, not as a kinship based on bodily descent.

Herder presented his principle in four theses. Because of their consistency and clarity, I will parallel these with Linnaeus' four statements on the fixity of the species. Just as Linnaeus furnished in those statements a closed system of axioms for the structure of each species, Herder posited a system of axioms for the arrangement and subdivision of the diversity of species. The first of these four propositions reads: "The classes of creatures increase, the further they are removed from man; the nearer they are to him, the fewer are the genera of the so-called more perfect animals."[11] This statement refers to the fact of experience that the number of species increases when organisms are arranged in descending order from the most perfect to the lowest. The second proposition establishes the law of "the one principal form," according to which all living beings are formed. Herder even expands this statement beyond life-forms and considers it possible that even the structures of the subliving world are organized according to the same "building plan" as those of the living world.[12] The second principle states that "as they come closer to man, all creatures in their major forms more or less resemble him, and in spite of its infinite diversity, which it loves, nature has apparently formed all living things on our earth in accordance with One Principal Plasma of organization."[13] This proposition is based on the morphological kinship of living beings, as shown by comparative anatomy, and claims that a series of decreasing similarities from man to the lowest forms can be established.

The third proposition states that "each specimen explains the others." The species are variations on a building plan, and each one embodies certain parts of the basic plan more clearly and more completely than another and vice versa, so that only all species together are the complete manifestation of the plan. "All the beings of the or-

11. Johann Gottfried von Herder, *Ideen zur Philosophie der Geschichte der Menschheit*, 57.

12. *Ibid.*: "In the gaze of the eternal being, who views all things in one connected whole, perhaps the form of the icy particle as it is generated and the flake of snow that grows on it may have an analogous relationship to the formation of the embryo in its mother's womb."

13. *Ibid.*

ganic creation therefore appear as *disjecta membra poetae*. To study them, one must study each one in the others."[14]

The fourth proposition establishes man as the "excellent middle creature, in whom the most numerous and subtle rays of similar forms are gathered, as far as is consistent with the singularity of his destiny. . . . Were we to compare with him those animals that are nearest to him, we might almost venture to say that they are refracted rays from his image, reflected through catoptric mirrors."[15] As an intermediate creature, Herder suggests, man is the elaborated form in which the traits of all species around him are gathered in refined form.

The whole of living creation is the analogon of One Organization, and the organisms are arranged in an orderly series according to their distance from the center, from man; the greater the distance from him, the more nature had to deviate from its model.[16]

In another context, on the occasion of the classification of races, we have already spoken about Herder's theory of man [*Menschenlehre*] and of man's place as intermediate creature between the purely animal and the purely spiritual life. The concept of the intermediate creature, intermediate member, or intermediate ring that

14. *Ibid.*, 58–59.
15. *Ibid.*
16. *Ibid.*, 60. Goethe's theory of the "type," which corresponds to Herder's "principal form," by his own admission goes back to the close contact with Herder. Anatomical studies compelled Goethe to propose a type by which all mammals were to be tested according to whether they were congruent with it or differed from it. Just as Goethe had made efforts to find the primordial plant, he also sought the "primordial animal," the "idea of the animal." "My arduous, painful research was made easier, yes, sweetened, in that Herder undertook to set down the *Ideen zur Geschichte der Menschheit.* Our daily conversation dealt with the primal beginnings of the watery world [*Wassererde*] and the organic creatures that have developed on it since time immemorial." This passage is found in *Morphologie,* in the section "Der Inhalt bevorwortet," of 1817 (*Goethes Werke,* Cotta, XXXII, p. 10). The typology is drafted in the section "Über einen aufzustellenden Typus zur Erleichterung der vergleichenden Anatomie," the second of the lectures on *Entwurf zur allgemeinen Einleitung in die vergleichende Anatomie, ausgehend von der Osteologie* (1796). The idea is formulated in "Metamorphose der Tiere"

> Alle Glieder bilden sich aus nach ew'gen Gesetzen,
> Und die seltenste Form bewahrt im Geheimen das Urbild.
>
> [All members are formed along eternal laws
> And the rarest of forms secretly preserves the primal image.]

On Goethe's conception of nature, see the treatise by Kurt Hildebrandt, *Goethe und Darwin: Eine Hundertjahrbetrachtung zum Siege der Naturwissenschaft über die Philosophie* (Archiv für Geschichte der Philosophie, XLI).

occurs there must not be confused with the concept whose meaning we have analyzed just now. The double meaning of this "intermediate" concept arises at the juncture of two trains of speculative thought. The first summarizes the law of the physical diversity of the organic world while the second formulates the essential difference between animal and man. Depending on whether we relate the development to the physical part of man or to man as a spiritual whole, we encounter entirely different problems, which, for speculative reasons already known, cannot be combined into one. The methodological incompatibility between a biological investigation of man and an anthropological one that studies man as a spiritual whole recurs in every subsidiary problem of the issue. Thus, although the problems of the morphological order in the organic realm and of the ontological series that extends through several areas of being cannot be joined together, Herder makes this effort, with the result we already know and for which Kant in his review so emphatically rebuked him. Herder continued the series of physical forms beyond the human *soma* into the figure of the human spirit, and this step results in a radical change of the subject matter. While the ascending orderly arrangement of animal species revealed the higher unfolding of natural forces—though in such a way that each individual animal lived and died on the level it occupied and only a different *species* stood on the higher level—the study of man gave rise to a concern for the *singularity of the person,* and the orderly series underwent this strange break because there is no level of higher beings following upon that of man; instead men rise individually to the status of a fully developed humanity, freed from earthly shortcomings. In the following chapters dealing with the internalization of the person, we will pursue the idea of the unified form and its development in more detail.

§4. The Immanent Factual Order of the Series (Kant)

In the repeatedly cited review of Part I of Herder's *Ideen* of 1784, Kant briefly comments on the question of development as it would have to be answered from the standpoint of the idea of immanence, even though he himself still felt this answer to be overly bold. Herder's and Goethe's principles of a factual order of the world of organisms are, as I said, on the way to an immanent formulation of the law, but they do not quite reach it because the principle revealed in the orderly arrangement of the various bodily forms is one outside the body itself [*leibjenseitig*]. Organic forms are the analogues of a building, but they neither create nor vary the plan by themselves. Therefore, Kant objects to Herder's classification of forms based on their similarity to each other and to the human form on the grounds that the empirically given similarity among organisms is a consequence of their rich diversity: given the great number of species and the small differences between them, it is little wonder that they can be arranged according to similarity, but from that it does not necessarily follow that there is a common building plan for all. "Only a *kinship* among them, by which either one genus descended from another, and all from one single original genus, or perhaps from a single creative womb, would lead to ideas, which however are so outrageous that reason shrinks from them, such as, without being unfair, one may not attribute to our author."[17] A few years later Kant already felt more at ease with this "outrageous" idea though he still had reservations, and in the *Critique of Judgment* he considers it at length. By then he no longer considers similarity a natural consequence of diversity and sees pursuing the question in more detail as not entirely pointless. He explicitly declares "praiseworthy" the efforts to trace morphological kinships with the help of comparative anatomy in order to find a system and a principle of creation. From the similarity in the building plans of so many animal species he draws the hope that in time genuine insight into nature on the basis of mechanical principles will be possible. "This analogy of forms, insofar as despite all their diversity they seem to have been produced according to a common original image, strengthens our supposition that there is an actual kinship between them through their descent from a common first mother, through the gradual approach of one animal genus to the next."[18] This ladder, Kant conjectures, extends from man down to the lowest animals and, through plants, to the lowest level of nature, the raw matter from which all of living nature seems to have descended according to mechanical laws. Many speculations are possible about the course of this development: how the "womb of mother earth," having only just emerged from chaos,

17. Kant, Review of Herder's *Ideen*, I.
18. Kant, *Kritik der Urteilskraft*, §80.

initially gave rise to creatures of less expedient form, and how these in turn gave rise to others more suitably formed for their environment and their relationships among each other until finally this womb became petrified and from then on limited its births to definite species that were not further modified, and the diversity of nature remains as it was at the end of the activity of that fertile formative force. The theory of the descent of the species is fully developed here, even including, as an explanation for the current fixity of the species, a theory of the former, now extinct, fertility of the productive force, such as Georges Cuvier was to advocate subsequently. Nineteenth-century theories of evolution, especially Darwin's, added factual details to Kant's theory and improved it by removing many objective difficulties, but they changed nothing in the basic framework. On the other hand, compared to Kant's theory, the theories of the nineteenth century actually represent a huge step backward on account of the decline of theoretical culture and the consequent naiveté with which relatively insignificant details are considered important and lauded as progress in treating the question, while the crucial speculative-theoretical basic questions are overlooked.

§5. Life as Primary Phenomenon

Kant deals briefly but thoroughly with these crucial questions in a few sentences appended to the well-meaning consideration of the possibility of a real descent of species. He points out that if the radically immanent theory of evolution were accepted, researchers would have to ascribe to the universal mother, with her generative power, an expedient organization geared to all the creatures that have come forth from her and without which the appropriate forms of the animal and plant worlds would be impossible. "They have then only pushed the basis of explanation further back and cannot claim to have made the development of those two kingdoms independent of the prerequisite of ultimate causes."[19] In this one sentence the idea of the inner law of evolution is carried to its conclusion—at the same time that its theoretical significance is blunted. The turn to the theory of evolution has the *theoretical* goal to *ex-*

19. *Ibid.*

plain the building principle [*Baugesetz*] of each species based on the preceding evolution of species. If this idea is followed to its logical conclusion, the law according to which species develop moves closer and closer to the beginning of the history of evolution, until the first life-form is endowed with the evolutionary tendency for the entire living world, and finally speculation pushes back beyond the first life-form into inorganic matter, from which the former spontaneously originated. The "explanatory" law that was intended to be immanent thus turns again into a transcendent one, into a law that "precedes" the evolutionary series of life. And the types of organisms, the species, in spite of their supposed historical descent from each other, nevertheless stand again side by side, inexplicable through each other since the conditions for the development of any one species cannot be found in the one that precedes it historically and generationally, but only in the law that stands outside the whole series of species. The attempt to "explain" the species leads to the unexpected result that the species once again stand side by side as fixed types, similar to the way Linnaeus saw them, even though in reality they may be related to one another through genesis.

We have come to the end of our investigation of the transformation of the idea of the transcendence of evolution to that of immanence. Just as for the organic individual his structural law, the immanence of his being, could not be replaced by the preformist theory of the series, just as there the problem of infinity had to be resolved within the species in order to arrive at the finite concept of the individual life-form's formative drive, so in the theory of evolution the doctrine of the descent of species must be dissolved as the explanation of the individual species, so that the idea of the fixity of the species, of the immanent law of the species form, can be found again. The theoretical situation is only less transparent in evolutionary theory than in the infinite series of species. While in the latter we only had to trace the dissolution of the concept of series to arrive at the immanent concept of the organism, in evolutionary speculation we had to (1) investigate the transformation of evolutionary theory from the transcendent to the immanent idea, as it ran its course from Leibniz to Herder, Goethe, and Kant; and (2) see, behind the evolutionary theory's becoming immanent, the dissolution of its explanatory law all the way to the reappearance of the fixity of the species. Kant's argument that the theory of evolution merely shifts the real origin of the species back to the origin of evolution not only takes the theory of evolution to its logical conclusion but also destroys it as meaningless as far as its explanatory purpose is concerned. It does not explain what it was intended to explain, in fact, it explains just as little as Leibniz' principle of continuity or Herder's or Goethe's idea of morphological kinship. The kinship relationships of the living world are primary phenomena just as the life of the species and the life of the individual organism are primary phenomena, which one can see or not, but there is nothing about them that needs to be explained. The primary phenomenon of life becomes visible in a threefold way: in the living individual, in the species, and in the interconnectedness of the entire living world. It is impossible to use a part of this phenomenon to explain the same phenomenon in another of its manifestations. The life of the individual cannot be explained through the life of the species, as the theory of series has attempted to do; the life of the species cannot be explained by the totality of the phenomenon of life, as the theory of evolution attempts to do; and the totality of the phenomenon of life can most definitely not be explained through the laws of non-living nature. In the substantially genuine movement of the spirit, the theory of evolution has come to an end in the *Critique of Judgment*—although in the history of derivative theories on this issue, theories that move ever farther away from the center of the spirit, evolutionary theory did not flourish until the following century.

Kant appended a note to his radical destruction of the explanatory value of any theory of evolution in which he conceded that the *fact* of bodily kinship was not impossible. It was not, he remarked, totally absurd and a priori impossible that, for example, certain water animals might gradually evolve into marsh animals and, after some further generations, into land animals. "However, experience gives no example of it; according to experience, all generation that we know is *generatio homonyma*. This is not merely *univoca* in contrast to the generation out of unorganized material, but it brings forth a product that is in its very organization like the one that produced it; and *generatio heteronyma*, so far as our empirical knowledge of nature extends, is found nowhere." This sentence, written in 1790, still applies word for word today; biology has nothing to add to it.

B. THE INTERNALIZATION OF THE PERSON

15

Immortality of the Person
and Perfection of Generic Reason

Given the conclusions of the previous chapters, we can also call the topic of the internalization of the body the disentanglement of the tangle of constructions, so that a view of the primary phenomenon of life itself opens up. Now we must continue with a similar process to disentangle related constructions until we obtain a clear view of the primary phenomenon of the human form in the fullness of its physical-spiritual [*leiblich-geistig*] totality. On the level of thought images this transformation is again expressed in a subversion of the dualism of reason and body until we attain the concept of the human person as a unified, unbroken being, who is neither spirit without body nor body without spirit. Thus on a higher ontic level, the problem of the organism recurs. Here again the schema of the duality of matter and mind must be laboriously overcome to make room for the notion of the indivisible unity of the mode of being that is sought. Concerning the internalization of the body, we were dealing with a vitalization [*Verlebendigung*] of matter, without straying into hylozoistic theories or analogies with artifacts or into purely external combinations of a piece of matter with an individual *anima*. Concerning the internalization of the person, we are dealing with making sensory [*Versinnlichung*] an immaterial intellectual principle without sinking into a materialization of the psychic. The object is to attain the idea of the finite whole, of the body or person, from the two poles of matter and soul, body and spirit. In the case of the organism making the idea sensory is making it finite, a withdrawal from the speculations about infinity, and the same applies also in the case of the person. The person, up to this point conceived of as an immortal substance, is now, as a result of its internalization, to be understood as finite, this-worldly; it is to be understood on the basis of its own intrinsic laws.

We will take up the problem at the place where Kant dealt with it, although it has a long and great history prior to that. The mathematical aspect of the problem of the infinite basically had already been elucidated by Leibniz, though neither he himself nor thinkers of the late eighteenth century drew the appropriate conclusions regarding the treatment of the problem of the person. In Leibniz' letter to Bernoulli of August, 1698, cited earlier, we find the statement: "Sane ante multos annos demonstravi, numerum seu multitudinem omnium numerorum contradictionem implicare, si ut unum totum sumatur." [Many years ago I have completely demonstrated that the number or multitude of all numbers implies a contradiction if it be construed as one whole.] The infinite amount of numbers is already clearly seen as a contradiction in terms by the end of the seventeenth century, but for a number of epistemological problems pertaining to the infinite an appropriate analysis was not provided until Kant's antinomies, and even here the issue of infinity as applied to the person remains entirely unsettled. Leibniz had posited the monads, including those endowed with reason as uniquely created and indestructible until the total annihilation of the world. And throughout the entire eighteenth century, whenever a rationalization of the problem of the person is attempted, we still find a doctrine of infinity that typically assumes either the Christian form of an immaterial afterlife in the beyond or the form of the transmigration of souls, the repetition of finite existence for an infinite number of times. The most significant German formulation of the question before Kant seems to me to be Lessing's, enunciated in *Die Erziehung des Menschengeschlechts* of 1780. Humanity as a whole in the infinity of its being is to be led to the goal of love and virtue for its own sake; over an infinite period of time humanity is to be brought up to a final state of perfection. But how can this challenge for mankind as a genus be reconciled with the meaning of the confined, finite existence of the individual? Does the individual's life then have no meaning, and is only the totality to be guided to perfection? Lessing solves the question by assuming an infinite migration of the individual immaterial soul. The whole progresses by imperceptible steps, and the large, slow wheel that brings humanity closer to the goal is moved by the small cogs of the finite lives. "Each individual person (one sooner, the other later) must first travel the path by which the whole race [*Geschlecht*] arrives at its perfection." The in-

148

dividual ego may repeat its existence as often as it is destined to ac-
quire new knowledge and skills; all of eternity lies before it, and
over this time it can perfect itself along with the race; thus, the perfection of the genus coincides with the perfection of all individuals
through the series of their rebirths.

"Life" here is altogether incorporeal, substantially simple soul,
in its permanence no different from the elements of inanimate matter, and we now see more clearly why Kant could call the organism
only an analogon of life and had to distinguish it from life itself
when the latter is conceived of as a lasting substance, unlike the already elaborated finite concept of natural purpose. The same observations made about the problem of infinity in the sequence of numbers and the series of preformed germs would now have to be
repeated for the series of soul migrations. Nor should their "eternity" be taken as a *totum*, as something concretely given, as an infinite process of perfection, for all events lose their meaning when
they are conceived of as infinite. An infinite process of perfection is
synonymous with an absolute standstill for any finite intuition, for
every finite step on the way and every finite phase of perfection are
infinitely small in relation to the whole when the latter is seen as
something infinite. Every finite stretch on humanity's path of education, no matter how big we envision it to be, cannot show any perceptible change if the measure of change is taken from an infinitely
large one. The idea of the whole universe [*Weltganzes*] as the unity
in which the perfection of the ego takes place necessarily destroys
the meaning of the finite life of the person in his earthly existence.

Faced with this problem in his philosophy of the person, Kant
tried to find a solution in *both* directions marked out in the schemas
indicated above. First, by assuming the immortality of the individual person as the precondition for the infinite approximation of perfect virtue, second, by assuming an infinite historical process, in
which the human race is led to its goal under the guidance of providence. In both solutions Kant finds himself compelled, in view of
the break between finitude and infinity, to express his astonishment
at the emerging inconsistencies—both times in a way that allows us
to look deeply into the mysteriousness of the situation.

Kant considers individual immortality essential so that man
may attain the highest good, which consists of the harmony between his happiness and moral perfection. Man is split into his na-

ture and his rational person, which is subject to the moral law, and concerning his finite life one cannot foresee how the satisfaction of his nature is to coincide with the fulfillment of the moral law, whose requirements are completely independent of man's nature. "*Happiness* is the condition of a rational being in the world, in whose whole existence *everything goes according to his wish and will*. It thus depends on the harmonizing of nature with his entire purpose which is equivalent to the essential determining ground of his will."[1] But the moral law has dominion over freedom, without any consideration for nature: "Hence there is not the slightest reason in the moral law for a necessary connection between the morality and the proportionate happiness of a being belonging to the world as one of its parts and as such dependent on it."[2] The necessary and appropriate connection between virtue and happiness, however, is the highest good that we as sensory-rational beings must set ourselves as the task of our will; and the foremost precondition for realizing this highest good is again "the complete appropriateness of our basic convictions to the moral law."[3] However, "complete appropriateness of the will to the moral law is *holiness*, a perfection of which no rational creature in the world of senses is ever capable. But since it is nonetheless required as practically necessary, it can be found only in an *endless progressus* heading toward that complete appropriateness; in accord with principles of pure practical reason, it is necessary to assume such a practical progression as the real object of our will."[4]

According to Kant, however, this infinite progress is possible only if the existence and personality of rational beings continue on into infinity; the immortality of the soul is therefore a postulate of pure practical reason. The attainment of the highest good, the coincidence of happiness and virtue, lies in the far reaches of infinite personal existence and is not possible in a finite existence. Kant was so completely imbued with the truth of this train of thought that he was astonished that philosophers could even entertain the possibility of this-worldly perfection and fulfillment [*Sinnerfüllung*] of exis-

1. Kant, *Kritik der praktischen Vernunft*, 124. All quotations are taken from the edition of the Philosophische Bibliothek, Meiner; page numbers are from the Akademie edition.
2. *Ibid.*
3. *Ibid.*, 122.
4. *Ibid.*

tence. "When we see ourselves compelled to seek at such distance —namely in the connection with an intelligible world—the possibility of the highest good, which reason presents to all rational creatures as the goal of all their moral wishes, it must appear strange that philosophers of both ancient and modern times have been able to find happiness with virtue in very proper proportion even in *this* life (in the world of the senses) or, at any rate, have been able to persuade themselves that they had."[5] Based on his assumed contradiction between sensory existence and reason in earthly life, Kant considered the finitist observation on personality pointless. The essence of man, Kant maintained, consists of his intelligible rational personality, and as long as this is bound to man's nature, it cannot exclusively influence his volition [*Willkür*]; the tendency to follow one's drives [*Trieb*] can never be completely excluded. Only God's will is holy and as such not capable of any maxims that contradict the moral law. "For rational but finite beings, only unending progress from lower to higher levels of moral perfection is possible. The Infinite Being, for whom time is nothing, sees in this progress, which for us is endless, a whole appropriate to the moral law; and holiness, which his law inexorably demands in order to be fitting for his justice in the share of the highest good he assigns to each, can be found in a single intellectual intuition of the existence of rational beings."[6]

Thus the problem of the finiteness of existence is changed because the sensory nature of man's earthly being is seen as only a symptom of finiteness, not its constituent, for the person does not lose any of his finiteness when he dies and lays aside his sensory body. Life in the hereafter is not perfect all at once just because it is freed of its earthly fetters; rather, it is also a finite existence in contrast to the one infinite existence of God. The complication of the problem through the question of man's sensory nature is resolved, and the essence of his finiteness is placed in the development of the person through an infinite becoming; what for divine intuition is a unified, self-contained substance, resting in its perfection, can only be understood by finite human beings in the infinite process. The incomprehensible disintegration of being in time, which becomes

5. *Ibid.*, 115.
6. *Ibid.*, 123.

complete and whole again in God's eternity, is for Kant—as it was for Augustine—the formula in which he expresses the nature of finiteness. From the necessary parallels of temporal disintegration and divine eternity follows his astonishment at attempts to get a finite view of the whole of the person.

Independent of the treatment of the infinity problem in the schema of individual immortality, Kant uses the second schema to pursue the inquiry into the infinity of the progress of the whole genus' reason toward the goal of perfection in the course of world history. Lessing harmonized the infinite perfection of the individual with the meaning of the development of mankind as a whole by basing the education of the human race on that of all individuals through the sequence of their rebirths. If Lessing's thought is taken to its logical conclusion, both series collapse into one since the human race in history is not an infinite sequence of different persons but a chain of appearances of always the same persons. The questions of the perfection of the reason of the genus and of individual reason cannot lead to a conflict. Kant, on the other hand, isolates the two series from one another, but without resolving their internal connection in the concept of universal reason, and that is why the situation of "astonishment" arises again for him in historical observation.

The statements in *Idee zu einer allgemeinen Geschichte in weltbürgerlicher Absicht* develop the axiomatics of Kant's theory of person and history with outstanding rigor. The basic axiom is that of the dual nature of man as member of an animal species and as member of a species of rational beings. The meaning of an animal's life is completed in its finite existence; it has no faculties for any other purposes than those of its life between birth and death. In man, the rational being, however, the natural abilities aiming at his use of his reason are destined, according to Kant, to develop fully only in the genus, not in the individual. Since we should not think of nature as playing without purpose (otherwise, instead of lawfulness, we would see before us nothing but desolate chance [*Ungefähr*]), the object of man's striving must be the complete development of the faculties nature as a wise providence has bestowed upon him to the idea of man; since one human life is evidently too short to develop all faculties, an infinite series of generations is needed to unfold all of them. Only in this series of humanity does reason reach its goal.

Man must bring forth everything that transcends the mechanical ordering of his animal existence out of himself, under the guidance of his reason, and he should not share in any other perfection (as the animal does in its instinctual happiness) but only in the one gained freely, without instinct, through the activity of his own reason. Great difficulties for man lie ahead on this path, but nature was apparently less concerned about his welfare and more about his worthiness for the happiness he is to gain through his striving.

What remains astonishing in this is that the earlier generations seem to carry out their laborious activity only for the sake of the later ones, namely, to prepare for them a level on which they in turn can raise higher the edifice intended by nature; and that only the last generations are to have the happiness of living in the edifice on which a long series of their predecessors have worked (though unintentionally) without themselves having been able to share in the happiness they prepared. Nevertheless, mysterious as this may be, it is indeed also necessary once we assume: an animal species is to have reason and as a class of rational beings, who all die, but whose species is immortal, they are to arrive at the perfect and complete development of all their faculties.[7]

7. Kant, *Idee zu einer allgemeinen Geschichte in weltbürgerlicher Absicht*, end of the third statement.

16

The Problem of the Finite Person; Specialization by the Division of Labor; the Elite and the Masses

Formal principles of the formation of the sequence of events, problems of the ontology of man, and very concrete questions of everyday life in Kant's time, all contribute to creating this philosophical situation. The principle of the formation of series is the development of the reason of the kind, envisioned as universal, toward a final state of perfection along the road of the development of its particularities [*Besonderungen*] in the individual human rational substances. Now, since the series of the species and that of the individual cannot be united by a theory of transmigration of souls, there arises at the intersection of species and individual being the astonishing situation that the individual and his achievements are merely a means to the end of the perfected life of the last generations. Though the idea of immortality takes care of the perfection of the individual, perfection in the next world nevertheless seems to Kant not sufficient to wholly offset happiness in this world. Thus, keeping these aspects of Kant's ideas together, the result is the somewhat muddled situation that our earthly life is by nature so imperfect that it must appear "astonishing" that any philosopher could ever think it meaningful in itself while, on the other hand, this earthly life is nevertheless considered so perfectible that earlier generations seem to be at a decided disadvantage compared to later ones. There is no remedy in the Kantian system for these difficulties since the reason of the individual has the same structure as that of the whole species and the problem of uniting an image of human totality with the singular totality of the person is not yet clearly seen. Yet, we find the first, albeit still vague, signs of dealing with this problem in the concrete notion of the process of man's gradual perfection through the antagonism among all of the individuals' faculties. Man's natural "unsociable sociability" drives him to seek the society of others, not through gentle adaptation to others, however, but through showing off before others out of a thirst for glory and a craving for admiration. Inordinate ambition, the desire to dominate, and greed prompt us to develop all our talents. Even though our talents may be directed against other men, the whole process nevertheless stimulates the capacity of all men for cultural and civilizational achievements, and thus a whole is created out of the partial achievements competing with each other. La Rochefoucauld's and La Bruyère's empirical theory of man, Mandeville's idea of society, and Adam Smith's idea of a society based on a division of labor are the prerequisites for the Kantian idea that the conflict of individual powers and faculties, though fueled by dubious motives, nevertheless leads to a whole of ultimate value. The idea of the totality of humanity is certainly there, but it can be imagined only as a whole made up of fragments; the individual is not yet a self-contained personality, a meaningful unique existence in itself, but rather a particular kind of center of forces, one that develops its faculties one-sidedly, no matter how much this specialization contradicts the idea of man.

Specialization through the division of labor, particularization of human powers that prevent the individual from perfecting his humanity, this was the special problem of that time, and attaining the self-contained personality was its task. Schiller lamented the contrast between the all-around, well-rounded image of man of antiquity and the deplorable fragmentation of modern man. The image of the species, enlarged, is indeed refracted in the individuals—"but in fragments, not in altered mixtures, so that one has to ask around from individual to individual in order to gather together the totality of the kind. . . . What modern individual will step forward, man against man, to vie with the individual Athenian for the prize of humanity?" The fragmentation of the spiritual whole of society in the sense of the ancient polis touches all levels of emotional and intellectual life. State and church become separated, and so do laws and morality; speculation detaches itself from intuition and becomes independent; the arts and sciences become specialized and lose their connection through a common primordial ground; the simple relationships of the earlier republics, in which each person could develop his individuality fully and, if need be, return to being a whole, have given way to a complicated mechanism in which each office must be administered according to strict forms. "The dead letter substitutes for living reason, and a practiced memory is a safer guide than genius and sensitivity."

Yes, it is even damaging to a man's professional career when his powers exceed his tasks and the greater needs of his intellect drives the man of genius to be active outside his office. The individual concrete life is erased, so that the abstract life of the whole can eke out its miserable existence. Agreeing almost word for word, the poets lament; Schiller writes: "Forever chained only to a single small fragment of the whole, man develops himself only as a fragment; having in his ear forever only the monotonous sound of the cog he turns, he never develops the harmony of his nature, and instead of expressing mankind in his nature, he merely becomes an imprint of his business, his science."[1] And only a short time later Hölderlin's lament and hope are heard:

> Aber weh! es wandelt in Nacht, es wohnt, wie im Orkus,
> Ohne Göttliches unser Geschlecht. Ans eigene Treiben
> Sind sie geschmiedet, allein, und sich in der tosenden Werkstatt
> Höret jeglicher nur, und viel arbeiten die Wilden
> Mit gewaltigem Arm, rastlos, doch immer und immer
> Unfruchtbar, wie die Furien, bleibt die Mühe der Armen.
> Bis, erwacht vom ängstigen Traum, die Seele den Menschen
> Aufgeht, jugendlich froh, und der Liebe segnender Odem
> Wieder, wie vormals oft, bei Hellas' blühenden Kindern
> Wehet in neuer Zeit, und über freierer Stirne
> Uns der Geist der Natur, der fernherwandelnde, wieder
> Stille weilend, der Gott, in goldenen Wolken erscheinet.

> [But, alas, our generation wanders in darkness, it lives
> As in Orcus, without God. Men are bound to their own tasks
> Alone, and in the roaring workshop each can hear
> Only himself. They work like savages, steadily,
> With powerful, restless arms, but always and always
> The labor of the fools is sterile, like the Furies.
> So it will be until, awakened from anxious dreams,
> The souls of men arise, youthfully glad, and the blessed
> Breath of love blows in a newer time, as it often did

---

1. Schiller, *Über die ästhetische Erziehung des Menschen, in einer Reihe von Briefen*, 6th letter.

For the blossoming children of Hellas, and over freer brows
The spirit of nature, the far-wandering, shines for us again
In silent, lingering divinity from golden clouds.][2]

Behind fragmentation [*Zerrissenheit*] as the common evil of the
time, from which man must find his way back to a more noble unity
and formation of the personality, the special disaster of the forlorn-
ness of large masses of the people in dire need becomes visible, from
which no escape seems possible. The thought of an elite as the vehi-
cle of humanity begins to emerge; the exhortations intended to encourage the cultivation of humanity are directed only to this elite.
"The larger part of mankind is much too tired and worn out from the
struggle against need to rouse itself to a new and harsher struggle
with error. Satisfied with escaping the sour toil of thinking, that part
of mankind is glad to be under the tutelage of others for its ideas, and
if that higher needs should stir in it, it grasps with thirsty faith the
formulas which the state and the priesthood keep ready for the occasion." These unhappy people deserve only compassion, but those
others, whom a happier lot allows a brighter life and who submit to
the yoke of their needs only out of the laziness of their character and
the cowardice of their hearts, merit our just contempt.[3]

The gospel of the new humanity is addressed only to the few who
are not consumed by the hustle and bustle of everyday life and the
problems and necessities of life: "So it is really only a small number
in whom the desire, the urge, the yearning of the mind for self-
understanding makes up an essential and lasting dictate of their inner life, and it is to these, then, that the message of these pages is
addressed, always hoping that even in that mass that is at present
unreceptive, individuals will again emerge in whom the desire that
lies at the roots of everything will awaken again and compel them
toward this nourishment or actually into the depths of their own being."[4] A much broken line leads from these first insights into the
new structure of society and into the impossibility of making the demand for education a requirement for the masses to the theories of
Engels and Lassalle, according to which the increase in the productivity of labor as a result of technological progress will enable the

2. Hölderlin, "Der Archipelagus."
3. Schiller, *Über die ästhetische Erziehung,* 8th letter.
4. Carl Gustav Carus, *Psyche: Zur Entwicklungsgeschichte der Seele,* foreword to
the first edition (1846).

worker, too, to develop his humanity, and to Nietzsche's doctrine of the necessary servile condition of the majority of people in order to provide leisure for the few to create works of the mind, and to the elitist theories of the ilk of a corporatist or race theory, and directly to Stefan George's idea of the New Aristocracy, which must emerge from fragmented [*zerfallen*] humanity and gather around a new center for the formation of a New Reich.

Like Kant, Schiller believed that the antagonism among forces was the great instrument of culture, but unlike Kant he considered it nothing more than an instrument. Schiller was not satisfied with the idea of the infinite progress of this instrumental evolution; he wanted to see the result of a fully formed, noble humanity within a finite time period. Kant focused on all of mankind and did not want to give up as lost even one of its members and therefore held that only the genus as a whole could reach the goal of perfection in an infinite process. Schiller, on the other hand, had his eyes on the individual, the one raised above the masses, who would be able to develop the totality of his personality while the masses, at least for the time being, lagged behind the ideal. Schiller's idea veers off from Kant's rational construction of the democratic community in its history; out of his realistic view of the social problems of his day, Schiller subdivides humanity into the chosen few and the great mass of the disadvantaged. His astonishment, unlike Kant's, concerns not the notion that the present generations as a whole merely serve the future but rather the thought that the idea of the perfect life supposedly cannot yet be realized in at least some individuals. Although Schiller's statements agree almost word for word with Kant's, their intention heads in a completely different direction. Kant had his eyes on the community of *all* men, who were all moving *together* toward their goal; Schiller articulated the idea of the beginning of the future perfection of *all* through the perfection of *individual* persons in the present.

17

The Person of Goethe as Ideal; Schiller's *Letters on the Aesthetic Education of Man*

Kant and Schiller go their separate ways regarding the question of how it can be possible to rise from the present fallen condition to a better one. In this question Kant took a completely skeptical stance; he realized that the greatest problem of mankind was to unite the antagonism of forces in a bourgeois society administering the laws, but he did not know how to solve the problem that the enforcement of a system of laws requires of a ruler, and this ruler in turn must come from precisely this human species that is so imperfect as not to be able to live without a ruler. Where can man find this ruler? "Nowhere else than in the human species. But this person is at the same time also an animal who needs a ruler. No matter how man goes about it, it is impossible to see how he can find for himself a leader of public justice who is himself just. . . . This task is therefore the hardest of all; indeed, it is impossible to solve it completely; out of the warped wood man is made of, nothing truly straight can be made. Nature demands of us only our approach to this idea."[1] There seems no way out of this circle that the improvement of mankind's condition requires an already improved man to guide and encourage the others on the path to order and perfection.

It is concerning this problem, on which Kant remains skeptical though tending more toward pessimism, that Schiller introduces his idea of the person. "All improvement in the political sphere must start with ennobling character—but how can character be ennobled under the influences of a barbaric national constitution? For this purpose one would have to search out an instrument that the state does not offer, and open up sources for it that, in spite of all political corruption, run clear and true."[2] The way out of the circle is

1. Kant, *Idee*, 6th statement.
2. Schiller, *Über die ästhetische Erziehung*, 9th letter.

found with the introduction of an apolitical source of humanitarianism—a way that was not open to Kant because for him practical humanity was nothing more than the existence of man under the moral law out of pure reason, and the problematic of the infinity of the rational substance was precisely the basis for the circle. For Kant, finite reason was by nature corrupt and could never be the source of a pure, meaningful fulfillment [*Sinnerfüllung*] of earthly existence. But the idea of the perfect man, whose perfection of being in this earthly life could be the impetus for an improvement of human character in society, had become conceivable through the actual appearance of such a man, just as the theory of the antagonism of forces and the fragmentation of the community had been shaped by the reality of eighteenth-century society. The perfect man, who nourished hopes for a happier age, was Goethe.[3]

The ninth letter in *The Aesthetic Education of Man* contains the famous portrait of Goethe[4] in which the character of the great personality and the effect hoped for from it are depicted.

The artist, to be sure, is the child of his time, but so much the worse for him if he is also its pupil, or, worse yet, its favorite. May a beneficent deity tear the infant betimes from his mother's breast, nourish him with the milk of a better age, and let him grow to maturity under the distant Greek sky. Then, when he has become a man, let him return, a foreign figure, to his century; not to gladden it by his appearance but terribly, like Agamemnon's son, to cleanse it. Though he will take his material from the present, he will borrow the form from a nobler time—indeed, from beyond all time, from the absolute, unalterable unity of his being. Here, from the pure ether of his demonic nature flows the spring of beauty, uncontaminated by the corruption of races and times, which surge deep underneath it in turbid eddies.[5]

3. On Goethe's role as a leader, see Max Kommerell, *Der Dichter als Führer* (1928).

4. See also Schiller to Goethe, October 20, 1794:

I still have not put pen to paper concerning the political misery, and what I have said about it in these letters I said merely so as to say nothing more about it for all eternity; but I believe that the confession I have made here is not entirely superfluous. No matter how different the tools are with which you and I grasp the world, and no matter how different the offensive and defensive weapons we wield, I nevertheless believe that we are aiming at one principal point. In these letters you will find your portrait, to which I would gladly have appended your name, if I did not hate anticipating the feelings of thoughtful readers. No one whose judgment can have any value to you will mistake it, for I know that I have conceived it well and drawn it accurately enough.

5. Schiller, *Über die ästhetische Erziehung*, 9th letter.

All the conflicts of his time are sublated in this man; intuition and thinking are no longer separate functions; rather, "the highest that man can make of himself" is achieved since he has succeeded in generalizing his intuitions and in rendering his feeling law-making. The spring of beauty flows unsullied from the purity of his "demonic" nature. And the demon in his unity of the supreme human-being [*Mensch-Sein*] is the model of the "beautiful life" that can be led only by the "beautiful soul," in which sensory nature and morality are united. In the beautiful life, "as in a painting by Titian, sharp boundary lines have disappeared, and yet the full figure emerges all the more truly, vitally, harmoniously."[6] Rich in color, full and well-rounded in appearance, the image of the perfect man is conjured up—the man who has sublated within himself all conflicts and fragmentations of Kant's rational being. Freely and confidently the ideal emerges where the possible and the necessary intersect; through education the rational man turns nature into a friend not by despising or neglecting it but by respecting its freedom while yet curbing its capriciousness [*Willkür*]; graciousness is the expression of the soul in which duty and inclination harmonize; and the substantial unity of man is no longer reason but the demon of the great man, which Kant had not yet experienced as real.

Where and in what form can the community of the beautiful life, the "aesthetic state," become reality? This question can no longer be answered merely in regard to reason and its developmental possibilities, since sensory nature and reason have been united in the body-soul unity of the beautiful whole. The "Greek spirit" of Goethe points to the place where the image of the perfect man was first realized—to Greece.

There, where a gentle zephyr opens the senses to every gentle touch and where an energetic warmth ensouls luxuriant matter—where the kingdom of the blind masses has already been overthrown in lifeless creation and where victorious form ennobles even the lowliest natures—there, under the cheerful conditions and in the blessed zone where only activity leads to pleasure, and only pleasure to activity, where holy order wells up from life itself and only life develops out of the law of order—where the imagination flees reality forever and yet never strays from the simplicity of nature—here

6. Schiller, *Anmut und Würde*, p. 273, in *Werke* (Cotta, 1867), XI.

alone senses and spirit, receptive and formative powers, will develop in the same happy harmony that is the soul of beauty and the precondition for humanity.[7]

The aesthetic mood of the mind owes its existence not to man's freedom of reason; rather freedom is actually a result of this mood; the flowering of the beautiful soul is a gift of nature—only the latter may, thanks to the benevolence of chance, loosen the fetters of sensory existence and lead chained man to the freedom of beauty. Schiller's idea of nature has become just as heavy with the sensory-bodily, accidental-unpredictable creative power as Kant's concept of nature was marked by the image of a purposively guiding providence.

Schiller's concepts present a characteristic stage in intellectual history for the development of a new thought: what is newly seen cannot yet be made concretely accessible to others simply by naming it, because the audience does not yet associate the name with the thought connected to it. The name must be made clear, on the one hand, by referring to something concrete everybody knows (in this case by pointing to the person of Goethe) and, on the other hand, by relating the name clearly to the concepts that have been handed down. In the case of the concept of the organism, we saw how it emerged gradually, by means of the analogies of the mechanism, the artifact, the immaterial life-forms, all of which it was *not,* until its position was finally found to be defined at the intersection of the notions that, on the one hand, leaned to the lawfulness of nature (Kant) and those that tended to anthropomorphic forms (Goethe). Now, in the internalization of the image of the person, we find that the first stage of the new concept's definition is its local determination at the point where two concepts, presumed to be familiar, intersect, namely, sensibility and reason. The complete man is no longer to be envisioned as determined either by the senses or by reason, but rather as a new unity in which the individual-asocial incommunicable element of sensory nature is united with the one that is absolutely the same for all men—the reason belonging to species as a whole. The individual thus becomes the "representative of the kind"[8]—that is, he becomes a being joined to all others through the community of the genus but nevertheless represents this universal-

---

7. Schiller, *Über die ästhetische Erziehung,* 26th letter.
8. *Ibid.,* 27th letter.

ity in a particular way. The concept of the "representative" of humanity is a first step toward overcoming the dualistic fragmentation of man into a natural and a rational half, but it is not more than just a first step. The individual is seen as a unified being but still as one specimen among many others, not yet as a unique being, a singular person.

As in Kant, the totality of man as unified, though not unique, leads to the image of a community of equals called the state. Except that this state is no longer a "dynamic" one, in which man meets man as a force of nature; nor is it an "ethical" one, in which people are mutually bound by their duties; rather, corresponding to the new harmony of these contradictions, it is an "aesthetic" one, in which men as free "figures" are connected to each other socially. This aesthetic state is not in itself hierarchically ordered according to significance and rank of the singular persons participating in it; instead, it is just as much a community of equals as is Kant's cosmopolitan community. It differs essentially from Kant's community only in the fact that it is not a regulative idea for the living together of all people that can be realized only in a far-distant future but rather is a real, existing, current structure, in which a human elite is already united today. "According to need, it exists in every soul of a sensitive mood [*feingestimmt*]; in fact, it is likely to be found, like the pure church and the pure republic, only in a few select circles, where behavior is guided not by mindless imitation of other people's manners but by one's own beautiful nature, where man strides through the most complicated conditions with bold simplicity and calm innocence and neither needs to wound other people's freedom to assert his own nor to throw away his dignity in order to demonstrate his charm."[9] Though the democratic construction of the community of equals is broken by the idea of the "select circle" (Goethe's idea of the "smallest company"), within this circle the singular persons do not yet complement each other to form a subdivided totality; instead, they still stand side by side, analogously to the schema of equality proper to Kant's concept of the state.

9. *Ibid.*, end of the 27th letter.

18

Wilhelm von Humboldt's Concept of Individuality; The Force of Spirit

By characterizing Schiller's ideas as the typical first stage in the formation of a new concrete worldview [*Anschauungswelt*] of the nature of the person, I have already hinted at further stages of the influence of the person of Goethe as the great concrete image that serves as orientation for the movement to increasing internalization of the concept of the person.

Through the appearance and ever increasing visibility of the singular individuality of Goethe the force of the idea of the step-by-step, continuous advancement of humanity toward an infinitely distant goal was broken, though in part the constructive apparatus remained and was only gradually destroyed. Its dissolution began with Schiller, with the assumption that meaningful human life can be realized in the present in a select community modeled after the demonic man, who, drawing on unfathomable sources of strength, breaks through the oppressive reality of the fragmented present. This dissolution continues with Wilhelm von Humboldt's concept of individuality as a spiritual force that arises independent of the course of events and begins a new series; history does not extend from its beginnings into infinity as a homogeneous sequence of events linked by cause and effect; instead, nodal points form within it, and an explanatory science of history must pause at these. These nodal points are not ordinary transitional points in the course of events but independent sources of power; they absorb past events into themselves and release them again in a new configuration that can no longer be derived from anything prior to its point of origin. Though progress is noticeable in the course of events, this progress is not a purposeful rushing toward a goal but something that can be described only in terms of organic analogies. "Peoples and individuals proliferate vegetatively, as it were, like plants, spreading across the earth, and enjoy their existence in happiness and activity. This life that ends with every individual goes on undisturbed, without regard to effects for the centuries that follow; nature's decree that everything that breathes shall complete its course to the last gasp, the purpose of beneficently ordering goodness, that every creature shall attain to enjoyment of its life, these are accomplished, and each new generation undergoes the same round of joyous or painful existence, of successful or frustrated activity."[1] The appearance of man's spiritual force is sudden, not tied to progress or clearly bringing it about; its origin is inexplicable and its effect unpredictable; its highest manifestations are not necessarily the most recent. Kant saw the ideal of manhood in the person of Frederick the Great, and he saw in this figure a symptom of continuous enlightenment and a guarantee of humanity's further advancement to a higher form. And precisely in this he overlooked the singular greatness of the person, subordinating it to the idea of the infinite series as guarantee and proof of the correctness of his view of history. The person of Goethe now has a completely destructive effect on this view, allowing individuality to appear as a mysterious manifestation of a spiritual force, a life principle behind history. Though no connection between the individual manifestations is visible, its existence may be believed; the individual developments are not disjointed just because their outward manifestations are isolated.

This viewpoint is completely different from that of purposes since it does not proceed toward a set goal, but instead starts from a cause acknowledged to be unfathomable. Now it is this view that alone seems to me applicable to the diverse forms of human spiritual power since—if it is permissible to make this subdivision—the forces of nature and the almost mechanical progress of human activity sufficiently satisfy the ordinary needs of mankind, but the emergence of greater *individuality* in some persons or in populations, which cannot be explained through any sufficient derivation, then suddenly and unpredictably intervenes in that visible path, governed by cause and effect.[2]

The starting point for Kant's astonishment at the obvious incompatibility between finite and supraindividual meaningfulness is not

1. Wilhelm von Humboldt, *Über die Verschiedenheit des menschlichen Sprachbaues und ihren Einfluss auf die geistige Entwicklung des Menschengeschlechts* (Berlin, 1836), 6.
2. *Ibid.*, 8.

missing here, but it does not remain in the construction as an unprocessed foreign element; rather, it gives rise to the subjective turn of the description of the effect the experience of finitude has on man's mind. Man sees the course of his own life as separated from that of human destiny, but he does not therefore think his life amounts to nothing more than his function in history. Rather, this essential human experience is the occasion for separating the self-development of his person from the shaping of the world in which each in his circle intervenes independently in the larger reality encompassing him. Man develops the inwardness of his mind through the realization of this contrast, and this inwardness, as substance of the person, has become the occasion for positing that contrast. This inwardness affects man all the more strongly "because man regards not only himself, but all of his kind, as equally destined to a lone and lifelong self-development, and because therefore all the ties that bind one mind to another attain a new and higher significance."[3] Man's fate and that of mankind as a whole diverge, but their relationship is not one of constructive contradiction; instead, their opposition reveals, if not insights, at least glimpses of a higher interconnection. There can be no doubt of the meaning of the individual life, but precisely the most determined individuality and lonely reserve conveys an idea of an encompassing totality and raises to consciousness the essential social acts (Scheler) of our striving for it. The meaning of individuality points beyond itself to a new, expanded meaningfulness derived from the total context; the more definitely individuality is experienced, the more definitely the totality becomes the object of yearning, "since every individual bears within him the total human essence, though limited to one line of development." It is impossible for us to envision any consciousness other than the individual one. "But this striving and the seed of indelible longing implanted in us by the concept of humanity itself, will not let the conviction perish that separate individuality as such is merely a symptom of the limited existence of a spiritual being."[4]

The inner structure of human existence, which forms the point of departure for reflection here, is, just as it was for Kant, the finitude of existence and the experience of the continuation of events beyond

3. *Ibid.*, 25.
4. *Ibid.*

existence, but the form of the speculation has been changed under the impression of the person of Goethe: man is no longer an element in a series, analogous to a mathematical one, in which the question of the meaning of life appears only as an accidental one that disrupts the neat construction and astonishes; instead the human being now emerges in an inner view in which the essential structure of existence appears as its structure of meaning. There is no longer a connection between a nebulous, infinitely distant meaning of the perfection of the whole kind and a meaningless individual existence; instead, to the undoubtedly meaningful inwardness of the mind is added the inkling of larger contexts of meaning. In this process of finitization of the person, the latter is internalized and thereby becomes meaningful in all the details of its structure—even though this concept of meaning is still a very general one, which makes the very meaninglessness of existence into the revelatory experience of life's deepest meaning. The teleological inquiry that surveys the totality of the world from a standpoint outside man and sees individual existence as subordinate to a universal, economic category of purpose is abandoned in favor of a reflection on meaning that explores the structure of existence from the inside. The totality is no longer a concretely given series extending into infinity but a striving, a direction of our yearning in our only given existence. The objective schema of the series of speculation only appears now and then, as an afterimage—for example, in the statement, "How the existence of the individual, which comes to an end in this world, is united with the ongoing evolution of the whole kind—perhaps in a region unknown to us—remains an inscrutable mystery."[5]

Humboldt prepared the way for the inclusion of the body into the idea of individuality and its personal "development" [*Bildung*] more clearly than Schiller did. Schiller spoke of the especially favorable sensory conditions under which the aesthetic character matured for the first time. Humboldt, on the other hand, pursues in more detail the idea of the bodily foundation of the individual's spiritual achievements when he discusses the prerequisites for the highest fulfillment of the purpose of language: special strength and intensity of the spiritual power affecting language are required as well as a special fitness of the Spirit to the development of language, that is, spe-

---

5. *Ibid.*, 26.

cial clarity and concreteness of ideas, a strong and creative imagination and, finally, a very special, refined sensitivity for the harmony and rhythms of sounds, "which is where ease and agility of the speech organs and acuity and sensitivity of the ears are important."[6] Favorable bodily characteristics here become just as important as contributing conditions to individual achievement as are mental, intellectual, and spiritual faculties. The individual as the manifestation of spiritual force is singular—and indeed singular on all levels of existence, from the highest to the lowest, including the body.

6. *Ibid.,* 9.

19

Goethe's Person in the Work of Carus; The State of Being Well-Born

The idea of human individuality, of the self-contained total being, is carried to its conclusion by Carus. Spirit and body are no longer two opposing principles within the totality of the individual, serving more to disintegrate rather than build up its complete essence [*Wesensfülle*]. They have become complementary moments of the person, complementing each other in building up the whole. The body is no longer a lesser part, whose evil, instinctual, sensual influence on man has to be controlled and, if possible, suppressed by his better self, reason. The body is no longer an embarrassing earthly remnant that thwarts perfection. It has become the foundation without whose good constitution a wide-ranging and free unfolding of the spirit is impossible. Once again the figure of Goethe is the great ideal, and the relationships between body and spirit can be concretely shown in him. For Carus, the fundamental trait of the Goethean character is "the concept of humanly perfect health as the actual basis of his individuality."[1] By health he means here not merely that of Goethe the individual but also that of "the line that begat him"; the healthy line [*Stamm*], then, is no less important than the individual's fortunate disposition, since "how can a person be healthy when sick, shattered natures are at the roots of his existence!" As Carus describes it, "The competent, somewhat pedantic, but thoroughly distinguished and honorable nature of the father, the delicately humorous, genuinely feminine character of the mother who was more or less high-spirited and lively into old age, have laid a basis here that could well become the element for allowing an idea of life to express itself that at one time could prove itself in many respects one of the perfect blossoms of humanity; Goethe was indeed

1. Carl Gustav Carus, *Goethe, zu dessen näherem Verständnis* (1843), 76. Quotations taken from the new edition by Eberlein (Dresden, n.d.).

what is said of so many but what so few truly are—a well-born man."[2] Carus realizes the full implications of the idea of the well-born person, in a way that is far removed from the barbaric natural-scientific dogmatizations of modern eugenics, which narrows the concept to apply only to particular physical conditions.

The state of being well-born and healthy of which Carus is speaking here is the capacity of a bodily-spiritual total being to respond to spiritual as well as physical diseases by eliminating the "organism of the disease." Carus, himself a physician, interprets disease as the growth of a new foreign idea of life alongside the one that forms the higher spiritual core of a person's life and its manifestation. The new foreign idea of life subjugates all life processes to its own nature and redefines their purpose according to its own, so that "a new peculiar life history runs its course in its own way and is completed within this organism's original own life."[3] The life of this disease may run its course without harming the existence it has taken over and may soon die out; on the other hand, it may overwhelm that existence, or, though the disease dies off, it may leave something deformed or atrophied behind in the organism, a "corpse of the disease," as Carus calls it. The well-born person is able to overcome his diseases, as Goethe often did, most clearly in the case of Werther, whose history of illness and healing is so completely and transparently presented in *Wahrheit und Dichtung*. "In a strange way this primordially spiritual [*urgeistig*] nature cast out again the diseased materials that life brought to it, with indefatigable vigor he subdued the war ever and again aroused in him, as in any man of mettle, in various ways by the small demons of this sublunary world, and with an unremitting striving he labored to continue building up his own inner structure to make it ever more distinguished, more handsome, and more powerful. All this taken together will make it understandable nowadays what I meant when above I spoke of the health of his nature as the fixed and most essential element in Goethe's individuality."[4]

Beyond the example of Goethe, Carus relates the works of the spirit to the healthy and diseased body, and in doing so he articulates an idea that has had many ramifications in various directions in modern psychology. I only want to point to the psychology of Nietz-

2. *Ibid.*, 77.
3. *Ibid.*, 81.
4. *Ibid.*, 98–99.

sche and his wide-awake and trenchant capacity to search out the spiritually diseased roots of ideas and works or the studies in psychopathology that uncover the relationship between mental creation and labile, tension-filled, and diseased spiritual lives. Carus anticipated a good deal of all this and captured it in a few sentences. Thus, when he speaks of "literators" ["*Literatoren*"] and poets who opposed Goethe, he means that the behavior of these people can be explained by sharper insight into the conditions of their inner life. This would show "precisely how closely what they call their poetry has always been and still is connected to the condition of their bodily life, which is variously consumptive, or hypochondriacal, or poisoned by dissipation, or atrophied through and through."[5] The "opposition" of the diseased spirit to the well-born one is due to the spiritual condition [*Seelenlage*] Nietzsche called *ressentiment* and which Klages translated so wonderfully into German as *Lebensneid* [life envy], thus bringing it closer to its vital root. While the works created out of inner sickliness produce a sense of unease and discomfort in the reader, from a work arising out of inner health and force of spirit, Carus continues, its vital breath of life wafts toward us. "When we are clear on our way of feeling, we can thus often tell even in retrospect from the impression a work has on us whether it was created by a healthy or a diseased character. We can then ourselves be the gauge from which we read the prognosis for a mind that could at one point develop only precisely these products."[6]

The physical-psychical connections Carus sees are organized in various ways. The foundation is "energy,"[7] a vital force that is both sensory and spiritual and that is an inherent part of every life from the start. Those who have an abundant supply of this energy can wrestle the "demons" besetting them to the ground; for those less fortunate their original existence will waste away—which is expressed in the sickliness of their productions and in *ressentiment*. Wherever the original life force is weak and is constantly at war with the organisms of disease growing within it, this vital struggle is reflected in the brokenness of their work. "Who would not have been able to guess, in the case of Lord Byron, in how many respects the dark realm of his mighty work was only the reflection of the destruc-

5. *Ibid.*, 78.
6. *Ibid.*, 79.
7. *Ibid.*, 88.

tive fire of an inner disease that had already crippled him early on, cast on the night sky of his poetry like northern lights?"[8] And finally, the soul expresses itself directly in body stature, in gestures, and in facial expressions. Goethe was not only "healthy," but also "someone who was handsomely and powerfully organized." "His upright bearing, his noble figure, his smiling lips, his forceful eyes, and the enchanting flow of his speech" were envied every bit as much as his great works. "Wit, sharp humor, worldly understanding [*Weltverstand*], and a thousand kinds of skills may often be manifested in a small, paltry, even deformed organization, but such a powerful attitude, such a world-historical productivity as Goethe's are practically impossible in a paltry and even in a merely ordinary bodily constitution, they require—indeed, to put it properly, they actually create a distinguished and beautiful physical shape."[9]

Here, too, the connection between body and soul is understood not as a dependence of the soul on its physical foundation but rather the other way around, as a building up of the body by the energy of the psychical life. But even this reversed relation of dependence is not stated unequivocally since Carus intends "energy" not only as spiritual but also as a vital force. In his theory of the state of being well-born the idea of an intimate unity of the spirit and the body in which it lives is attained, that is, the complete internalization of the person, as a manifestation of the spirit [*Darleben*] in a concrete existence. From the vantage point of this idea, which is directly evident in Carus' works, we can understand all the race theories of the nineteenth and twentieth centuries in their possibility. Only after the ideas of separate, autonomous existence of the parts of the total human being, body and mind, had lost their power and the idea of the total being had become concretely visible in the person of Goethe could the question concerning the consequences of body-soul unity for the spiritual achievements of man be raised in a meaningful way. Carus himself drew the direct conclusion from his insights for race theory in his sketch for a division of human races, starting with the experience of the person of Goethe.

8. *Ibid.*, 78–79.
9. *Ibid.*, 99.

20

Carus' Race Theory

Carus' essay on the unequal aptitudes of the various human races [*Menscheitstämme*] for higher spiritual development appeared as a commemorative publication on the occasion of Goethe's hundredth birthday.[1] In view of Goethe the man, inevitably the question had to be raised, "how precisely this individual and *only* this individual" came to be so gifted with "such a wealth of ideas, such an abundance of events, such powerful accomplishments."[2] How can the individual stand so far above the many? The question is answered by the insight that variety is part and parcel of humanity and its evolution. If humanity were an aggregate of countless minds of equal constitution and with equal aptitudes, it would indeed be incomprehensible why so many thousands go through life in the darkness of spiritual and worldly insignificance, while only one is destined to intervene beneficially and to such an extent in the history of his nation and to complete his existence in such a beautiful way. However, Carus argues, humanity is not an aggregate but an organic whole composed not of identical but of diverse elements. The higher and more perfectly the organism is built, the greater must be the variety of its parts. In the highly developed organism of society, all members are in a relationship of higher "reciprocity." And this reciprocity, the nature of which consists of give and take, an exchange among the members, would have to cease if all parts were alike—"a frightening dream, torment and horror of the soul."[3] Man's total being is encompassed by the organized inequality of body and soul, not only of the external figure but also of each separate faculty for higher spiritual

1. Carl Gustav Carus, *Denkschrift zum hundertjährigen Geburtsfeste Goethes: Über ungleiche Befähigung der verschiedenen Menschheitsstämme für höhere geistige Entwicklung* (1849).
2. *Ibid.*, 1.
3. *Ibid.*, 5.

development. The task of understanding this assemblage of inequalities, Carus continues, is fulfilled initially and approximately by delimiting larger groups of varieties, by subdividing people according to race or tribe, class, social status, character, and temperament.[4]

Carus was familiar with several race classifications. He mentions, for example, those set up by Blumenbach, Rudolphi, and Bory St. Vincent, and he knew already the first seven volumes of Klemm's history of culture. But he is not satisfied with these because the principle of classification in each case remains more or less superficial— skull shape, hair texture, and the like—and because none places people, as part of humanity, in relation to the landscape assigned to the human race as its abode, the earth. He replaces these classifications based on external physical traits with a grouping based on the relationship of the earth to the sun and the resulting four phases of day, night, dawn, and dusk.[5] Accordingly, humanity is subdivided into four groups of night peoples, day peoples, and eastern and western twilight peoples [*Dämmerungsvölker*]. According to Carus, this "non-material subdivision" coincides happily with the empirical one, so that the night people coincide with the Ethiopian race, the day people with the Caucasian or European, the dawn peoples with the Mongolian and Malaysian, and the dusk peoples with the American tribes.[6] These races can be ranked in such a way that the least capacity for spiritual development is found among the night peoples, the highest among the day peoples, with the twilight peoples occupying the middle. Though this subdivision is inadequate empirically and the classification principle's convincingness is questionable, the underlying attitude informing this attempt is crucial for the possibility of a race theory developing. In Herder's *Ideen* we encountered the idea that the unity of meaning of organic life transcends this life, permeating even the earth's structure and thus uniting it with the forms it bears into a formation of unified style. In Ludwig Ferdinand Clauss' theory, the most recent attempt at a race theory, we find attempts to develop the same idea empirically on the basis of photographs intended to document the expressive connection among countenance, body shape, the animal world,

4. *Ibid.*, 6.
5. *Ibid.*, 13.
6. *Ibid.*, 14–15.

and the landscape.[7] Here, in Carus, we see the first system of a subdivision into races in which the totality of all existing races is to be deduced, as it were, from definite, analogous subdivisions of elemental phenomena.

As always in Carus, this idea must not be understood as claiming that the subdivision into races is dependent on inorganic, elemental natural phenomena. Carus' thinking is always focused on man as a whole from the diversity of whose bodily forms one can expect a priori that due to its content of elemental nature it harmonizes with the latter's organization. The whole being of man is nevertheless governed by spirit. The subdivision into races is not a bodily one to which is appended a typology of souls, as happens in modern race theory; instead, Carus tries to derive the possibilities of typological subdivision from the inherent lawfulness of mind and character. Thus, in contrast to the types of soul "traits" of Günther and Lenz, for example, Carus' types are based on a characterology that was, by the standards of his day, superbly elaborated, and the types can be understood only on that basis. Here we cannot even begin to outline the wealth of Carus' views on soul, person, and character; the treasure that has lain hidden here for so long is now being raised again—especially through the efforts of Klages. We can only touch on one detail to show the kind of typology on which Carus bases his classification of races, namely, his views on the growth and rigidification of the mind:

It is very important for the psychologist to pay attention to how exceedingly different the *scope* of spiritual development is in different people, how certain minds stop developing very early on, very soon arrive at a certain rigidity where further development, new creative efforts, and fervent assimilation of something foreign are no longer possible, where only what is customary and has already been attained remains valid and effective, and where any desire to try one's hand at something new ceases completely. Conversely, there are other individuals whose mind remains supple, never fully comes to terms with itself, is never finished with anything, and therefore also never entirely safe from error and uncertainty but is always tirelessly driven to move forward, to rush toward new metamorphoses, until at last it reaches a breadth and greatness to which, when they are combined with an inner truth and beauty, we have always owed all extraordinary

7. Ludwig Ferdinand Clauss, *Von Seele und Antlitz der Rassen und Völker: Eine Einführung in die vergleichende Ausdrucksforschung* (1929).

achievements for mankind as a whole. There has always been much strife and conflict between these different characters, and all the more so, the more fundamental the difference at work here is and the less it is thus due to any coincidental, external circumstances and the more it is due to original inner disposition.[8]

This is the passage to which the remark concerning race theory refers: "The difference presented here, which any observer of humanity will have many opportunities to apply and which thus serves to assess the character of many different individuals correctly, can also be applied to entire peoples."[9]

In describing the types in detail, Carus applies the general principles of his theory of the soul. By virtue of its higher nature, the mind is not meant to stand still, and if it is true to its nature, it does not stop its growth prematurely, as the body does. The Kantian idea of the series continues to resonate in Carus' words about an infinite path open to the mind and on which it must progress, now more slowly, now more quickly. Tireless activity is in the nature of the mind. The characteristic thus defined can now serve to form types: concrete human groups either correspond to the "active" type or deviate from it, ending their activity prematurely and succumbing to rigidification. The day peoples belong to the first type, the eastern twilight peoples—especially the Chinese—to the second. At the same time this sort of typology also ranks each type by value. The type that perfectly corresponds to the nature of the mind occupies a higher level than the one that deviates from it. Carus can therefore say of the active type, "Though being aware of such restlessness may at times lead to great torment, more frequently it redounds to great happiness, and if we think of everything great and significant that humanity has brought forth, for the most part we ultimately owe it precisely to this restless drive."[10] The inhibited development of body and spirit, on the other hand, seems to us to be a standstill, a closing off, a rigidifying, and therefore defective, even monstrous. "There can be no doubt that concerning the Chinese, this best explains how *that* could develop in them what perhaps might best be called the *overall rococo* of humanity."[11] What is disconcerting

8. Carus, *Psyche: Zur Entwicklungsgeschichte der Seele,* 2d ed. (1st ed., 1846), 270–71.

9. Carus, *Denkschrift,* 62.

10. *Ibid.,* 63.

11. *Ibid.*

about a standstill and the shaping of forms in which no life moves any more is the alienation from the true nature of the spirit. Constant transformation, tireless growth, these are what distinguish the human from the animal soul. The style of rigidification lets man slide back into the twilight between the two realms.

There is a considerable distance between the notions of the human norm held by Buffon and those Carus developed. For Buffon, a particular human type was the normal one, from which all others visibly deviate to a greater or lesser extent in both body and mind. Carus developed the norm from the nature of the mind and tests empirical types to discover if they come more or less close to the norm. For Buffon, deviation from the norm was an oddity, a curiosity, an exotic marvel that might arouse astonishment or compassion but nothing else. For Carus, the inequality is of necessity grounded in the nature of humanity as an organism. The idea Schiller developed—that only select groups embody the ideal of humanity, while the rest of mankind is still very far removed from this level—informs even Carus' race theory. The relationship between unequal men and groups of men, that is, the races, is one of reciprocity, of exchange and support. Though the tribe of the day peoples has the right to regard itself as the "proper flowering of mankind," at the same time it is also obligated "in part to serve as a beacon to the weaker, in many ways disadvantaged tribes and in part to stand by them everywhere as helper and to prove useful."[12]

The cited passages and the short comparative references to earlier ideas show the numerous threads that converge in Carus' race theory. Knowledge of the diversity of bodily forms is only one of its preconditions; to this is added the internalization of the concept of man and all the phases it has undergone. The idea of closely relating the human races to the shape of the earth was already possible for Herder, though he still considered the expression *race* to smack too much of the animal realm; compared with the body the mind was still strongly differentiated, and the equality of everything with a human countenance was not yet jeopardized. The theory [*Lehre*] of the uniqueness of each human being, who must find his own happiness in his earthly life and is not meant to be a mere dependent element in the total progress of humanity, had not yet advanced to the

12. *Ibid.*, 85.

degree of sociality we find in Carus' work. For this the additional mediating step leading from Kant's idea of humanity through the view of the person of Goethe to Schiller's idea of the beautiful life and its realization in small circles was needed. The net of a theory is here woven out of many threads, a theory distinguished less by its conceptual keenness and its proof in the empirical material than by the breadth of mind and the depth of insight with which Carus fathoms the world.

While Carus' thinking represents the endpoint of a major development, it also reveals the directions future thinking on the phenomenon of races was to take. The impetus for discussing the subdivision into races was the view of the person of Goethe. This unique man, this towering figure, was visible to all, and for Carus race theory was a first step toward exploring the inequality of men in general, which is evident in such differences in rank. The great individual was only possible when supported and surrounded by an outstanding race—namely, the day peoples. That one race so far outshone all others was the reason why the individual outshining all others necessarily had to come from this race. Race theory was to help us understand "how such a powerful individuality as that of our Goethe could emerge only from one tribe, which in itself was already a higher one and which therefore generally already promised its members an outstanding and powerful spiritual development."[13] Among the diverse races, one begins to stand out that fulfills the meaning of mankind most completely, and for Carus it already has the traits that today belong to the image of the Nordic race, although for Carus the race thus singled out still included all European and Near Eastern peoples. Eighteen groups make up the day peoples, among them not only the Persian people, the Pelasgian people, the Neo-Latin nations, the Celts, and the Germanic people, but also the Semitic people. The distinguishing achievements of these peoples are their migrations, the colonization of the Greeks, the early modern travels of exploration, their settlements all over the globe. The group of the day peoples, according to Carus, is the most richly subdivided, having the greatest number of pronounced national individualities, and therefore it rises more strongly than all the others

13. *Ibid.*, 7.

above the level of the organic into the truly human realm of unique personalities. The cultural accomplishments of these peoples surpass those of all other races: they have produced the greatest variety of languages; they have achieved great things in art and science; they have developed the means of transportation; they have invented tools; and they have exercised power, based on ingenuity and knowledge, over all other tribes. Though Fritz Lenz and H. F. K. Günther go into greater detail in delineating Nordic types, the fundamental features are nevertheless already outlined here. Even in the more subtle traits we find surprising analogies to current descriptions. In his book on the Nordic soul, Ludwig Clauss speaks about the moments of peak experience of Nordic man, locating them in the instant shortly before a battle is decided, even if the end is death; he uses the phrase "high tide in decline."[14] Carus speaks very similarly of the Greeks—they were the first to have a feeling for the beauty that is destined to reveal itself in man's life, indeed even in his death: "*That* is unique in history!—What other people would have written an epitaph for its fighters fallen for the fatherland of quite so *beautiful and human* significance as the remarkable lines:

> Those who died here, they saw beauty not in life or death,
> But in that both were accomplished *beautifully*."[15]

These reflections of Carus lead us right into the center of the race idea as a political idea shaping the community—a topic that lies beyond the scope of our inquiry here. We have investigated the systematic content of the race idea and the historical construction of that idea of man that is presupposed in modern race theory; now we see how the race idea becomes effective in the construction of the community—effective in the two intimately connected ways of objectively constructing the community through the idea of race and of subjectively convincing the people involved in the community that the race is essential for their connectedness as community. Race is no longer merely the object of scrutiny, seen at a distance; but a body-soul-spirit reality that includes the scholar himself, and the concept of race that is formed in the concrete situation is no

14. Clauss, *Die nordische Seele* (1923), 191.
15. Carus, *Denkschrift*, 94.

longer a scientific concept but a tool for interpreting the meaning of one's own life and the broader life of the community. It is not merely the creation of a passive attempt at "understanding," but an instrument in the service of the future shaping of the community; it is the idea of the community as a bodily context as it is projected into the future by its members.

Index